YOU ARE
NEXT IN
LINE

YOU ARE NEXT IN LINE

Everyone's Guide for Writing Your Autobiography

Armiger Jagoe

Capital Careers & Personal Development Series

CAPITAL
BOOKS, INC.
Sterling, Virginia

Capital Books, Inc.
P.O. Box 605
Herndon, Virginia 20172-0605

ISBN 13: 978-1-933102-60-3

Library of Congress Cataloging-in-Publication Data
Jagoe, A. L. (Armiger L.), 1921-
  You are next in line : everyman's guide for writing an autobiography / Armiger Jagoe. — 1st ed.
       p. cm. — (Capital careers & personal development series)
  Includes bibliographical references.
  ISBN 978-1-933102-60-3 (alk. paper)
  1. Autobiography. 2. Biography as a literary form—Study and teaching. I. Title. II. Series.

  CT25.J345 2007
  808'.06692—dc22

                                                    2007033942

Printed in the United States of America on acid-free paper that meets the American National Standards Institute Z39-48 Standard.

First Edition

10 9 8 7 6 5 4 3 2 1

This book is dedicated to all of us seniors, wherever we are. We are a marvelous group with bushels of life stories worthy of being recorded. In writing our personal histories, we are embracing the future by celebrating the past.

As 83 percent of those participating in my Next in Line program experienced both physical and mental improvement, my goal is to have no seniors left behind in using this unique technique for writing their autobiographies.

CONTENTS

Introduction

I wish I knew more about my family. When I review my personal history, it's like trying to assemble a jigsaw puzzle with many of the pieces missing. And the missing pieces are nowhere to be found.

The saga of a family is like a collage with its own unique pattern and colors. The life of each relative who has gone before is part of the overall picture. Because I know so little about my ancestors, my family collage is limited and has many voids.

For example, my father was a splendid father. However, my sister and I know about him only what we find in newspaper accounts of his successful banking career and his public service. He was a very private person who never talked about his parents, his siblings, or anything from his childhood. Being typical young people, we were too self-absorbed to ask him about himself.

What a treasure it would be if I could bring my father back to life for just one evening. There are so many things to ask him that we would talk until dawn. But I know that will never happen.

My wife, who is Spanish, has the same problem regarding her family background. Her English father was born in Barcelona where there was a large family business. When the Spanish Civil War broke out in 1936, he evacuated his wife and daughters on a British warship. He and his brother remained in Barcelona and occupied the abandoned British consulate.

For the next six months until he was ordered out of the country, my father-in-law forged hundreds of English passports, enabling endangered Spaniards to escape. Several of those he rescued were priests. This fragment of history is secondhand information because he didn't record his experiences during that period when the Communists confiscated his possessions and threatened his life. Now this noble man and those of his generation are no longer with us.

Having reached the age of eighty, I see clearly the importance of my relatives who have preceded me. In his or her way, each has contributed to my being. If I knew more about those whose genes I've inherited, I would have a better understanding of myself.

It always delights people when a genealogist reports having found an ancestral grain of greatness in his or her lineage. The *piece de resistance* for the genealogist is to locate, somewhere in the dim past, the suspicion of a drop of royal blood, legitimate or otherwise.

Although a genealogy report provides names, dates, and a few facts about past relatives, it lacks the lifeblood of an autobiography. Only the person who is the protagonist can tell the tale with depth of experience. For that reason, it is imperative for those of the older generation to record their lives for the benefit of the younger members who will be entrusted with family heritage. As next in line, you have the obligation to document the presence of the past.

As you begin writing your autobiography, remember this advice from Eudora Welty: "It's the doing of it that gets it done."

So, let's get started.

1

Why Me?

I have never met anyone over the age of twelve who didn't think that one day he was going to put down on paper the story of his life. The quest for some form of immortality is one of our inherent traits. As Mark Twain said, "Inside all seasoned *Homo sapiens* there is a desire to write about themselves."

Attesting to this truth, in writing about himself, Twain joined a long line of historic figures whose lives, taken together, form the fingerprint of civilization. Who is important enough to be written about? Do we need to be Julius Caesar or Katharine Graham to qualify? The brief answer is no. Every life is important because it adds a layer of knowledge to the human spirit. In your own way, you have influenced the world. And the recording of your life will be a sequel to all the other autobiographies.

This urge to write about one's self never goes away. Deep in the crevices of the mind, it's always there. However, most of us postpone writing our autobiographies until it is too

A life worth living is worth recording.

late. We keep putting it on the back burner. The problem is that it can't be done once the stove is turned off.

Time passes quickly. Suddenly, it's a shock to realize you're next in line to record your own life story. If you don't, it's everyone's loss. Writing an autobiography gives substance and meaning to a life that might otherwise be forgotten.

In family sagas, it's tragic to have knowledge gaps about those who have gone before. These gaps diminish the family as a whole, and valuable lessons and insights are lost forever. It need not happen.

Today, it's worthwhile to record yesterday so it can be appreciated tomorrow. And there are many reasons why you should begin today.

• *When you write your autobiography, you are acknowledging you are unique—one of a kind.*

Of the sixty billion people on earth, no one is precisely like you. No other person has a duplicate of your genes. No one else has had your experiences and observations. And even though you might be a persuasive person, others don't think exactly as you think.

Two centuries ago, in the introduction to his *The Confessions of Jean Jacques Rousseau*, the French philosopher wrote:

> I desire to set before my fellows the likeness of a man in all the truth of nature, and that man myself. Myself alone! I know the feelings of my heart, and I know men. I am not made like any of those I have seen; I venture to believe that I am not made like any of those who are in existence. If I am not better, at least I am different.

- *To get something done and have it done right, it's best to do it yourself—especially when it's the documentation of your own life.*

No one else knows the subject better than you. Therefore, you are the logical person to do it. The Hollywood legend Gloria Swanson said:

I'll be eighty this month. Age if nothing else entitles me to set the record straight before I dissolve. I've given my memoirs far more thought than any of my marriages. You can't divorce a book.

In his book *Presidents Who Have Known Me*, George E. Allen said:

Mine has been the kind of life that attracts autobiographers, but not biographers. To me it has been an extraordinary life, and I have long thought that somebody should write a book about it. And since I am the world's leading authority on the subject, I may as well do it myself. Then there is the further consideration that if I don't, nobody else will.

- *Although recording your history is a challenge, writing it will benefit you in many ways.*

Even if yours are the only eyes that will read your manuscript, by having done it, you will have become a more complete person. In studying a rerun of your life, you'll discover forgotten facts about yourself. You can find a therapeutic value in having to rethink both joyful and tragic events, and invariably you will find something new. Writing an autobiography is a rebirthing and should be honored.

Katharine Hepburn wrote in *Me, Stories of My Life*:

I am the main gift from my parents. And when I realized this, I also knew why I had suddenly become interested in writing this book. I wanted to discover the real back of all the fluff. That bit of fiber which can be developed in all of us— there it is, waiting to be used.

When I wrote my autobiography *Southern Boy*, I realized I had a time deletion of all but a few of the missions I flew during World War II. It was as if I had unknowingly erased something from my mental computer. When I discussed this with a friend who is a psychologist, he said that with hypnosis, I might recover these memories. When I told him I didn't want to bring them back, he smiled and said, "That's the reason."

•   *Writing your autobiography is the right thing to do.*

It confirms the truth of your existence, and it is a way of expressing appreciation for your loved ones and for the treasure of being. To acknowledge in writing the gift of your life is a nod of gratitude to the Supreme Being. Everybody likes to be thanked—even He.

2

Get Started

I had to go it alone. Before starting my memoirs, I bought every book I could find on the subject. To my disappointment, I found most of these publications were written by persons who probably had not written their own autobiographies. Their advice was as unimaginative as instructing a would-be artist to paint by the numbers.

Without inspired guidance, I had to wing it. I was like the bumblebee that doesn't know, according to aeronautics, that it can't fly. A year later, when I finished *Southern Boy*, I had learned a great deal that I could pass on to others planning to write their personal histories. I had been there and done that. With my experience, I have empathy for anyone who attempts the challenge.

The first concern most people have is how to record their story. Even the basic mechanics appear daunting. You have the choice of writing in longhand, typing (preferably on a computer), dictating, or talking into a tape recorder and having it transcribed. General Ulysses S. Grant

You will discover that your mind has a thousand eyes.

first insisted he would write his memoirs by hand. Near the end, when bad health forced him to dictate to a secretary, he was surprised how much he enjoyed doing this.

Vaclav Havel, former president of Czechoslovakia, and Fidel Castro, devastator of Cuba, agreed to tell their life stories by answering questions during interviews by professional journalists. Castro began by saying:

> And so, with absolute, total and sincere modesty, I accept the affection with which you have honored me this night, and the obligation to take on the horrible task of having to talk about myself.

"Courageous" Castro endured this horrible task by talking for twenty-four consecutive hours. His Brazilian interviewer, who described himself as a liberation theologist, hung in there. I hope they took time out to eat and go to the bathroom.

In composing your autobiography, don't be concerned about your ability to write. As talent lands wherever there's an available landing strip, you will find you possess writing skills you didn't know you had. If you can talk, you can write. Your manuscript will merely be your spoken words put on paper.

As you scrape away the rust, you'll find that memories start in your head and leap onto the page. Although writing often falls short of real meaning, you will create something beyond your expectations. You will discover that your mind has a thousand eyes.

Remember that those for whom you are writing will be concerned about content, not form. They want to know your facts, your thoughts, and your experiences.

Be honest, be direct, and your writing style will take care of itself. Rich simplicity makes for easy writing and enjoyable reading. And your account will lay claim on the imagination of the reader.

Flavor your story with the senses of color, sounds, and aromas. Ernest Hemingway instructed writers never to forget "the weather." In *Southern Boy*, I devoted a chapter to describing the sounds of my youth. This ranged from the slamming of the front screen door to the call of an ancient black man who used to drive his wagon along the beach road, selling fresh oysters.

I suggest you write in the first person. For example, "I did this, I did that, something happened to me." If you write about yourself objectively as a third person, you cramp your style. During times of antiquity, it was a common practice to write an autobiography in the third person. In 401 BC, the Greek historian Xenophon wrote of himself objectively when he narrated *The Expedition of Cyrus into Persia, and the Return of the Ten Thousand Greeks*. Only twice did he slip up and use "I." However, he very cleverly told of his heroic exploits by quoting himself. For example, he wrote:

> To meet these charges, Xenophon, in behalf of the soldiers, rose and said, "As to ourselves, men of Sinope, having got so far, we are well content to have saved our bodies and our arms. The rest of us, as you observe, are camping under the canopy of heaven, in regular rank and file, and we are ready to require kindness with kindness, but to repel evil vigorously."

Four hundred years later, Caesar referred to himself objectively in his account of *The Conquest of Gaul*. Around

1436, Margery Kempe also did this when she recorded her life story. In writing his autobiography, the famed architect Frank Lloyd Wright didn't refer to himself as "I" until he told of his college days.

You tend to restrict yourself if you write as someone else observing you. This makes it difficult to express your thoughts. You become removed, and this might tend to give a fragrance of fiction to what you want to be a straightforward account of your life. The Russian poet Anna Akhmatova warned that every attempt to produce a coherent memoir amounts to a falsification.

Be cautious about using the sketchy diary method in telling about yourself. Although writing a diary can be an effective means of recording details of the day, you risk cluttering your life story with nonevents. This device might be of value to a historian three hundred years from now. But in the meantime, you'll bore a lot of people.

Here is an example of the diary form used by Samuel Pepys in 1679:

> This day the wench rose at two in the morning to wash, and my wife and I lay talking a great while. I went to the White Horse in King Street where I got Mr. Buddle's horse to ride to Huntsmore to Mr. Bowyer's direction, and so took it into my mouth, which I found did me much good.

I thoroughly agree with the novelist P.D. James, who wrote in the prologue of her autobiography *Time to be Earnest*:

> A diary . . . is the most egotistical form of writing. The assumption is inevitably that what the writer thinks, does, sees, eats and drinks on a daily

basis is as interesting to others as it is to himself or herself.

Then, to prove her point when writing her memoirs she filled pages with dull trivia such as:

Saturday, 6th December. I arrived home in the early afternoon. Andy was waiting for me at Gatwick and drove me to Marks & Spencer on my way home to stock up with food. Polly-Hodge gave me her usual cool greeting to demonstrate displeasure at my absence, and then followed me around the house for the rest of the day. Everything was in good order. Joyce, with her usual efficiency, had sorted the post into matters requiring attention, those that were urgent and papers for information only. What on earth would I do without her? Next week is going to be exceptionally busy, but I shall think about that tomorrow.

In writing your life story, you have complete freedom in the way you join together the parts of your life that make up the whole. You can program your manuscript from birth to the present or vice versa. You can use the flashback technique.

But realize that there are a dozen elements of a successful autobiography. Regardless of how you structure your story, be sure to include each of the ingredients. When making bread, don't leave out the yeast. These essential components are:

1. *Purpose*
2. *Beginning*

3. *Family album*
4. *First home*
5. *Early years*
6. *Grown up*
7. *Adult life*
8. *Special people*
9. *Humor*
10. *Important events and life passages*
11. *Be kind*
12. *Reflections*

As the first step in preparing to write, I suggest you make twelve folders, one for each of these components. As you ponder the past, a multitude of thoughts will flood your memory. Jot down each remembrance and file it in one of the folders. When you get around to writing your manuscript, these notes will provide the foundation of your story.

In pondering the design of his personal history, Frank Lloyd Wright wrote:

Trying to be honestly autobiographical in writing these pages, telling only what is true, I see why all autobiography is written between the lines. It must be so. No matter how skilled the writer or spontaneous he may be, the implication outdoes his ability or undoes his intentions.

Autobiography is impossible except by implication. For the life of me, I cannot see why I recounted so many episodes that were far inferior to those I delight to remember and tell now. ...As I remember, the best of life is a becoming.

Now that you have made the commitment to write your story, find the most comfortable means to record your thoughts. If a job seems easy, it gets done.

Don't give a thought about writing skills. You'll create the story, and style will take care of itself. Write from the heart using your senses to give depth to your telling.

Compose your memoirs as if you were reminiscing with a close friend. And above all—enjoy!

3

Purpose Comes First

A wise person once said, "If you don't know where you are going, you're sure to get there."

Before you begin a project, it's important to understand why you're doing it. Knowing your purpose and keeping it in mind holds you on track. It also helps you complete the task. When purpose and commitment work together, you succeed.

The usual motive for writing a personal history is the wish to be remembered and appreciated. Everyone wants to avoid the bleakness of being forgotten. Memory of you should not be like footprints in the sand, washed away at high tide.

You don't have to be an egotist to write your autobiography, but without a bit of conceit, you wouldn't be inspired to write. However, be careful not to sink your autobiography with too much self-praise. Let the facts speak for themselves. In writing his life's story, an automobile executive

Knowing your purpose and keeping it in mind holds you on track.

implied that he was the son of Zeus. By boasting, he confirmed that his head was bigger than he was.

In addition to leaving your footprints firmly implanted, there can be many purposes for writing your autobiography. You might act as a historian in recording your experiences, which will be worthwhile tidbits in the chronicle of mankind. For example, Xenophon's intent in 401 BC was to record for posterity his account of the Greek battles in which he was a participant. Presenting himself as a spectator, he wrote:

> They had at their back other Persians also, armed with breastplates, as many as three hundred. As soon as they were within a short distance, they bade any general or captain of the Hellenes who might be there to approach and hear a message from the king. After this, two Hellene generals went out with all precaution. These were Cleanor, the Orchomenian, and Sophaenetus, the Stymphalian, attended by Xenophon, the Athenian, who went to learn news of Proxenus.

Another historian and military leader, Julius Caesar, also had a clear purpose when he wrote his account of the Gallic Wars. During this long period of fighting, he sent back his reports to be read in the Roman Forum. Caesar's desire was to keep the senators informed and to justify the cost of the military operation. Of equal importance, Caesar's *Commentaries* kept his image alive with both legislators and the people of Rome.

In 1436, although she was illiterate, Margery Kempe considered herself to be a most remarkable woman and a saint. In attempting to prove she had both qualities, she wore out three secretaries in completing her autobiography, *The Books of Margery Kempe*. In the introduction, she made it clear what her purpose was. In the third person, she dictated: "She told her life story to release the spiritual force within her."

If Margery had lived in the twentieth century, she would have been a woman of national reputation, probably with her own TV show. However, her qualifications for sainthood would be subject to question.

Two hundred years later, while he was in the Tower of London awaiting execution, King Charles I composed *The Pourtraicture of His Majesty, in His Solitude and Sufferings*. He wrote it to document his side of the story in his conflicts with Parliament and the Puritans.

Quite often the reason someone writes his autobiography is to have it as a legacy for his family and friends. Jimmy Carter dedicated his book *An Hour Before Daylight*:

To my newest grandson, Hugo, with hope that this book might someday let him better comprehend the lives of his ancestors.

In the beginning of the story of his life, Thomas Jefferson wrote:

At the age of seventy-seven, I begin to make some memoranda of dates and facts concerning myself, for my own more ready reference and for the information of my family.

Others intended that their autobiographies would be inspiring examples for future generations. Around 440, St. Patrick wrote:

Although I am imperfect in many things, I never-
theless wish that my brethren and kinsmen
should know what sort of person I am, so that
they may understand my heart's desire.

The famed novelist, historian, and activist Elie Wiesel
said in his memoir *All Rivers Run to the Sea*:

I have told the story and will tell it again, will tell
it forever, hoping to find in it some hidden truth,
some vague hope of salvation.

Almost a thousand years ago, in *The History of My
Misfortunes*, Peter Abelard wrote:

And now it should suffice for your sorrows and
hardships you have endured that I have written
the story of my own misfortunes amid which I
have toiled almost from the cradle. For so shall
you come to regard your tribulations as naught,
or at any rate as little, in comparison with mine,
and so shall you bear it more lightly in measure
as you regard it as less.

In his autobiography *My American Journey*, General
Colin Powell summarizes his inspiring story as a tribute to
his country:

Mine is the story of a black kid of no early prom-
ise from an immigrant family of limited means
who was raised in the South Bronx and somehow rose to become the National Security
Advisor to the President of the United States and
then Chairman of the Joint Chiefs of Staff.

It is a story of hard work and good luck, of occasional rough times, but mostly good times. It is a story of service and soldiering. It is a story about the people who helped make me what I am.

It is a story of my benefiting from opportunities created by the sacrifice of those who went before me and maybe my benefiting those who will follow. It is a story of faith—faith in myself, and faith in America. Above all, it is a love story: love for family, of friends, of the Army, and of my country.

Around 1552, Geronimo Cardano, the remarkable Italian physician, gave a modest purpose in writing about his life:

My autobiography, however, is without any artifice; nor is it intended to instruct anyone; but, being merely a story recounting my life, not tumultuous events, like the lives of Sulla, of Gaius Caesar and even of Augustus, who there is no doubt wrote accounts of their careers and deeds urged by the example of the ancients. So, in a manner by no means new or originating with myself do I set forth my account.

Two men recorded their lives, hoping it would improve the future. The first was Abba Eban, one of Israel's early leaders and statesmen:

My main satisfaction is that many people across the world may have learned from me that the Jewish story, with its culmination in Israel's statehood, is a brave and noble adventure. My road from London through Cairo and Jerusalem to New York and Washington and back to Jerusalem again has been long and eventful. Many lifetimes have been crowded into a few decades.

My hope is that the Jewish people will be enabled by its experience of freedom to rise beyond the sufferings of the past and the frustrations of history into the assertion of its unique spirituality.

More than a hundred years earlier, the other autobiographer who intended for his story to benefit mankind was Frederick Douglass, a former slave. He wrote:

Sincerely and earnestly hoping that this little book may do something toward throwing light on the American slave system, and hastening the glad day of deliverance to the millions of my brothers in bonds, faithfully relying upon the power of truth, love and justice, for success in my humble efforts and solemnly pledging myself anew to the sacred cause—I subscribe myself.

One writer wanted his story to document the era of his life, the other to give a history of his religious belief. In 1994, the celebrated scholar and writer Henry Louis Gates, Jr., stated:

I have written to you because a world into which I was born, a world that nurtured and sustained me, has mysteriously disappeared.

At the time our Civil War ended, John Henry Cardinal Newman wrote in his *Apologia Pro Vita Sua*: "What I held in 1816, I held in 1833, and I hold in 1864."

Another purpose for documenting your humanity might be to recall an old hurt and to try to erase it. In his autobiography, written in 1765, the French philosopher Jean Jacques Rousseau told of just such an experience, which occurred when he was a youngster. He was accused of having broken a lady's comb, which had been left on the fireplace in the kitchen where he was studying.

His family made a federal case out of this, even calling in an uncle to serve as the inquisitor. With childlike obstinacy, Rousseau protested his innocence throughout the ordeal. In his autobiography he wrote:

> It is now nearly fifty years since this incident took place, and I have no fear of being punished again for this same thing. When I write these words, I feel that my pulse beats faster. That first feeling of violence and injustice has remained so deeply graven on my soul that all the ideas connected with it bring back to me my first emotion; and this feeling, which, in its origin, had reference to myself, has become so strong in itself and so completely detached from all personal interest, that when I see or hear of any act of injustice, my heart kindles with rage.

Two famous Americans wrote their autobiographies for financial reasons. They needed money, and they were frank to admit it. In the introduction to *Personal Memoirs of U.S. Grant*, the general wrote:

> Although frequently urged by friends to write my memoirs, I had determined never to do so, not to write anything for publication. At the age of

nearly sixty-two I received an injury from a fall, which confined me closely to the house while it did not apparently affect my general health.

This made study a pleasant pastime. Shortly after, the rascality of a business partner developed itself by the announcement of a failure. This was followed soon after by universal depression of all securities, which seemed to threaten the extinction of a good part of the income still retained, and for which I am indebted to the kindness of friends.

At this juncture the editor of the *Century Magazine* asked me to write a few articles for him. I consented for the money it gave me; for at that moment I was living upon borrowed money. The work I found congenial, and I determined to continue it. The event is an important one for me, for good or evil; I hope for the former.

Pushed by the insistence of his friend Mark Twain, the General began writing his autobiography, which he completed just a few months before his death. A short time later, the publisher of his manuscript paid Mrs. Grant four hundred thousand dollars—in those days, a tremendous amount of money.

The other who realized the financial value of his autobiography was Mark Twain himself. In 1907, three years before his death, while vacationing in Bermuda, he wrote:

I do not need to stay here any longer, for I have completed the only work that was remaining for me to do in this life and that I could not possibly afford to leave uncompleted—my Autobiography.

Although that is not finished, and will not be

finished until I die, the object which I had in view in compiling it is accomplished: that object was to distribute it through my existing books and give each of them a new copyright of twenty-eight years, and thus defeat the copyright statute's cold intention to rob them and starve my daughters.

I have dictated four or five hundred thousand words of autobiography already and if I should die tomorrow this mass of literature would be quire sufficient for the object which I had in view in manufacturing it.

Although your autobiography may have a blend of several purposes, your overall goal should be to give enjoyment to your readers. In his criticism of Proust's narcissistic memoirs, Alexander Woolcott said reading it was like bathing in someone else's dirty water. Unlike Proust, you want your autobiography to have fresh appeal. If you take delight in recording your past, readers will sense your joy.

4

In the Beginning

Few of us have the gift of total recall. We aren't able to bring to mind everything that has happened to us. Often, rather than our blaming this on poor memory, the culprit might be a bad cerebral filing system. We know something is there, but it takes a bit of effort to recover it.

This might be the case when writing your autobiography, an unfolding of the past that will become new. Don't underestimate the need to tell what you can remember about your infant-to-kid span of life. It might require some quiet time for you to retrace the road back to your earliest years. But it's worth doing because you will be spinning straw into silk.

When you were born, your mind was a clean slate. Try and recall your first sense of consciousness. This initial awareness was something you first observed and took in.

In her *Reason for Hope: A Spiritual Journey*, the remarkable scientist Jane

You will be spinning straw into silk.

Goodall pondered where to begin telling about her life. She wrote:

> This is a story about a journey, the journey of one human being through sixty-five years of earth time: my journey.
>
> Traditionally, a story begins at the beginning. But what is the beginning? Is it the moment when I was born, with all the charming ugliness of the newborn human baby, in a hospital in London? The first breath I drew so that I could yell about the pain and indignity of my forced expulsion from the womb?
>
> Or perhaps we should go back to the first truly human creature that was born of ape-men parentage, or back to the first little warm-blooded mammal? Or should we go back and back through the mists of unknown time to when the first speck of life appeared on planet earth as a result of some divine purpose or cosmic accident?
>
> It will serve my purpose to begin, simply, from the time when I drew my first breath and screwed up my face to cry my first cry, on April 3, 1934.

In telling of their beginnings, two authors credited prenatal events for having a powerful effect on their lives. Another said his character had been determined by the hour of his birth. In her life's story, completed two months before her tragic death, the famed dancer Isadora Duncan wrote:

> The character of a child is already plain, even in its mother's womb. Before I was born my mother was in great agony of spirit and in a tragic situa-

tion. She could take no food except iced oysters and iced champagne. If people ask me when I began to dance I reply, "In my mother's womb, probably as a result of the oysters and champagne—the food of Aphrodite."

And in his autobiography Frank Lloyd Wright recorded the incredible account of his mother's premonition and determination after his conception:

> The boy, she said, was to build beautiful buildings. Faith in prenatal influences was strong in this expectant mother. She kept her thought on the high things, for which she yearned and looked carefully after her health.
>
> There was never a doubt in the expectant mother's mind but that she was to have a boy. Fascinated by buildings, she took ten full-page wood engravings of the old English Cathedrals from Old England, a pictorial periodical to which the father had subscribed, had them framed simply in flat oak and hung them upon the walls of the room that was to be her son's. Before he was born, she said she intended him to be an Architect.

To justify the way he turned out, in his memoir Fidel Castro put the blame on the clock. He wrote:

> I was born on August 13, 1926. If you want to know the time, I think it was around 2:00 in the morning. Maybe that has something to do with my guerrilla spirit, with my revolutionary activities.

Nature and the time of my birth must have had some influence, right? What kind of day it was and whether or not nature has anything to do with the lives of people. Anyway, I think I was born early in the morning. Therefore, I was born a guerrilla, because I was born at around 2:00 in the morning.

To recall your early years, search deeply in a relaxed state of mind. What was your first flash of consciousness? In writing my autobiography *Southern Boy*, I began with this account:

> I was two years old and slept in my mother's second floor bedroom with windows overlooking the Gulf of Mexico. My crib was near the side window facing east. One summer morning, as the earth rotated slowly towards the neighbor's house, the sun's rays flooded the room.
>
> As I lay in bed, aware of the warm glow illuminating my world, suddenly translucent balls with the reflective colors of a prism began to flash around me. I laughed with delight. When it was over and I could no longer see them, I shut my eyes to retain the joy of their visit.
>
> Fairies, angels or some other supernatural force that is attracted to the innocence of children might have caused this phenomenon. Perhaps it was the sunlight glancing off my eyelashes. Regardless of the cause, it gave me a joyful foundation on which to start accumulating a multitude of happy memories.

Similarly, H.L. Mencken could remember his first sensory perception. In *Happy Days 1880–1892*, he recalled:

> At the instant I first became aware of the cosmos we all infest I was sitting in my mother's lap and blinking at a great burst of lights, some of them red and others green, but most of them only the bright yellow of flaring gas.
>
> The time: the evening of Thursday, September 13, 1883, which was the day after my third birthday. The place; a ledge outside the second story front windows of my father's cigar factory at 368 Baltimore Street, Baltimore, Maryland, U.S.A., fenced off from space and disaster by a sign bearing the majestic legend: AUG. MENCKEN & BRO.
>
> The occasion: the third and last annual Summer Nights' Carnival of the Order of Orioles, a society that adjourned *sine die* with a thumping deficit the very next morning and has since been forgotten by the whole human race.

In his autobiography Carl Jung also gave a clear description of his first impression of the world around him:

> One memory comes up which is perhaps the earliest of my life and is indeed only a rather hazy impression. I am lying in a pram, in the shadow of a tree. It is a fine, warm summer day, the sky blue, and golden sunshine darting through green leaves.

The hood of the pram has been left up. I have just awakened to the glorious beauty of the day and have a sense of indescribable well being. I see the sun glittering through the leaves and blossoms of the bushes. Everything is wholly wonderful, colorful and splendid.

In recording his first remembrances and his infancy behavior, St. Augustine confirmed that babies haven't changed since 400 AD. He wrote:

Little by little I began to notice where I was, and I would try to make my wishes known to those who might satisfy them; but I was frustrated in this, because my desires were inside me, while other people were outside and could by no effect of understanding enter my mind. Often I did not get my way, either because people did not understand or because what I demanded might have harmed me, and then I would throw a tantrum because my elders were not subject to me, nor free people willing to be my slaves; so I would take revenge on them by bursting into tears.

In her autobiography, P.D. James clearly recalled this amusing experience when she was a toddler:

My first memory is of an incident when I was just learning to walk. . . . I must have been under eighteen months old and my mother had taken me to Winchester to stay with her parents. My grandfather, Edward Hone, was Headmaster of the Choir School, later to become the Pilgrims'

School, and the boys were taught in a special classroom block in the garden. Having broken free of my mother, I toddled into the classroom to be met by a burst of laughter from the boys. I remember that my grandfather was sitting at a high desk in front of them and came over at once to take me by the hand and pass me over to my mother, who came fluttering through the door full of apologies.

When they were beyond the toddler age, not yet ready for school, both Charlie Chaplin and Richard Nixon had these experiences that each recalled. In his autobiography, Chaplin wrote:

> One of my early recollections was that each night before Mother went to the theatre Sydney and I were lovingly tucked up in a comfortable bed and left in the care of the housemaid.
>
> In my world of three and a half years, all things were possible. If Sydney, who was four years older than I, could perform legerdemain and swallow a coin and make it come out through the back of his head, I could do the same, so I swallowed a half penny, and Mother was obliged to send for a doctor.

In his memoirs, Richard Nixon tells of his first accident that he clearly remembered throughout his life:

> My first conscious memory is of running. I was three years old, and my mother was driving us in a horse-drawn buggy, holding the baby brother

Don on her lap while a neighbor girl held me. The horse turned the corner leading to our house at high speed, and I tumbled onto the ground.

I must have been in shock, but I managed to get up and run after the buggy while my mother tried to make the horse stop. The only aftereffect of the accident was that years later, when the vogue of parting hair on the left side came along, I still had to comb mine straight to hide the scar that came from the fall.

Writing your autobiography is like giving a tour of your private estate. The beginning of your life is the entranceway. Make it appealing. Then your guests will want to see what lies beyond.

5

Family Album

To understand who you are, it helps to know who you have been. When your name was called at the gene pool, the cells that responded determined what you are. You had no control over this selection. It was programmed long before your conception. But it's good to know something about the progenitors who contributed to your attributes, physical and otherwise.

For most of us, our knowledge about our ancestors is as recent as the day before yesterday. Unless you are a genealogy buff, you probably don't have many facts about your family history beyond the past two generations. Few people place importance on these mounds of family dust.

Although it's true that we have all inherited the same basic genetic legacy, the genetic differences among the multitude of clans have strong implications. Future generations, who will appreciate your autobiography, will eventually be your family's ancestors. For that reason, it's practical for you to record what you know about

Future generations will eventually be your family's ancestors.

older relatives even if you go back no further than your grandparents.

You may be the only one who knows about these people. For your grandchildren, your grandparents are four generations ago. Recording the memory of those who came first is a means of thanking them for their contribution to the clan.

In 1771, when Benjamin Franklin was serving in England as an agent for the Pennsylvania Assembly, he began his autobiography in letters to his illegitimate son back in America. Franklin carefully recorded the research he had done on his family. He traced forefathers back more than two hundred years.

In 1740, Colley Cibber gave his autobiography a very long title. It is *An Apology for the Life of Mr. Colley Cibber, Comedian late Patentee of the Theatre-Royal.* In this book, he presented a good summary of his family background. He wrote:

> I was born in London on the 6th of November 1671, in Southampton Street, facing South-ampton House. My father, Gaius Gabriel Cibber, was a native of Holstein, who came into England some time before the Restoration of King Charles II to follow his profession, which was that of statu-ary, etc. The bassorelievo on the pedestal of the Great Column in the city, and the two figures of the lunaticks, the raving and the melancholy, over the Gates of Bethlehem Hospital, are no ill monuments of his fame as an artist.
>
> My mother was the daughter of William Colley, Esq., of a very ancient family of Glaiston in Rutlandshire, where she was born. My mother's brother, Edward Colley, Esq. (who gave me my

Christian name), being the last heir male of it, the family is now extinct.

In composing your autobiography, you might begin by telling about your father's side of the family. Rather than merely making a genealogical list of names and dates, write any personal things you know about your father's relatives. This adds spice to what otherwise might be a bland dish.

In the sixteenth century, when Geronimo Cardano wrote his life story *De Vita Propria Liber*, he recorded his ancestors back to 1180 when Milane Cardano was prefect of Milan. Then he gave a detailed description of his father. He wrote:

> My father, Fazio, was a jurisconsult. He went dressed in a purple coak, a garment which was unusual in our community. He was never without a small black skullcap. When he talked, he was wont to stammer. His complexion was ruddy, and he had whitish eyes with which he could see at night. Up to the very last days of his life, he had no need to use glasses.

Three authors had good things to write about their fathers. Another didn't. Margaret Thatcher, who, like Elie Wiesel and Mohandas Gandhi, came from a grocer family, recalled her admiration for her father. She wrote:

> I had grown up in a household that was neither poor nor rich. We had to economize each day in order to enjoy the occasional luxury. My father's background as a grocer is sometimes cited as the basis for my economic philosophy.

So it was—but his original philosophy encompassed more than simple ensuring that incomings showed a small surplus over outgoings at the end of the week. My father was both a practical man and a man of theory. He liked to connect the progress of our corner shop with the great complex romance of international trade, which recruited people all over the world to ensure that a family in Grantham could have on its table rice from India, coffee from Kenya, sugar from the West Indies and spices from five continents.

Before I read a line from the great liberal economists, I knew from my father's accounts that the free market was like a vast sensitive nervous system, responding to events and signals all over the world to meet the ever-changing needs of peoples in different countries from different classes, of different religions, with a kind of benign indifference to their status.

In effect, I had been equipped at an early age with the ideal mental outlook and tools of analysis for reconstructing an economy ravaged by state socialism.

In *The History of My Misfortunes*, composed by Peter Abelard in 1140, he wrote:

I had a father who had won some smattering of letters before he had girded on the soldier's belt. And so it came about that long afterwards his love thereof was so strong that he saw to it that each son of his should be taught letters even earlier than in the management of arms. Thus indeed did it come to pass and because I was his firstborn and for that reason the most dear to him, he sought with double diligence to have me wisely taught.

Elie Wiesel's relationship with his father is a very touching story. He recorded:

I never really knew my father. It hurts to admit that, but it would hurt him even more if I deluded myself. The truth is I knew little of the man I loved most in the world, the man whose merest glance could stir me.

As a child and adolescent I saw him rarely. Carelessly dressed, often preoccupied but always friendly, he spent the week in his little grocery store—where he enjoyed chatting with customers as much as selling them things and at the community offices where he quietly worked to assist prisoners and refugees threatened with expulsion.

The child within me refuses to let go of his grandparents, as the man I am refused to be separated from his father. My companion, my judge, or simply my guide, he never leaves me. It is to him I turn at times of doubt. I fear his verdict, I seek his approval. His encouragement is essential to me, and his reproaches hurt. How often have I changed course solely in order not to disappoint him?

On December 10, 1986, at the Nobel Peace Award ceremony, as I was about to deliver my acceptance speech in the presence of the Norwegian king and parliament, the diplomatic corps and the world press, I felt unable to utter a word, for Egil Aarvik, president of the Nobel Committee, had mentioned my father in his address. My lips moved, but no sound came out. Tears filled my eyes, the tears I couldn't shed so long ago.

In his autobiography, *It's Not About the Bike*, Lance Armstrong, the first American to win the Tour de France, had nothing good to say about his father.

The main thing you need to know about my childhood is that I never had a real father, but I never sat around wishing for one either.

I never knew my so-called father. He was a non-factor unless you count his absence as a factor. Just because he provided the DNA that made me doesn't make him my father, as far as I'm concerned. There is nothing between us, absolutely no connection.

I have no idea who he is, what he likes or dislikes. Before last year, I never knew where he lived or worked. Since I sat down to write about my life, though, I figured I might as well find out a few things about myself.

Unfortunately, last year's Texas newspapers traced my biological father and printed a story about him, and this is what they reported: his name is Gunderson, and he's a route manager for the *Dallas Morning News*. He lives in Cedar Creek Lake, Texas, and is the father of two other children.

My mother was married to him during her pregnancy but they split up before I was two. He was actually quoted in the papers claiming to be a proud father and he said that his kids consider me their brother, but these remarks struck me as opportunistic, and I have no interest in meeting him.

Next, record what you know about your mother's background. For example, my mother's family, of English ancestry, settled in Virginia before the Revolutionary War; then they moved to Mississippi where they were plantation owners. Today, in the family homestead, a two-story white frame house with columns, there's a plaque that reads, "From this house came seven sons of the Confederacy." It lists my grandfather, who at that time was a fourteen-year-old army scout.

In her autobiography, Katharine Graham gave this excellent portrayal of both parents:

> My father came from a distinguished Jewish family with roots going back many generations in Alsace-Loraine, France. It was a family that numbered many rabbis and civic leaders.
>
> On her father's side, my mother came from a long line of Lutheran ministers in Hanover, in North Germany, whose number included, at least in more recent times, not a few black sheep. The Ernst family was handsome, gifted, driven and, unfortunately, riddled with a tendency towards alcohol addiction. My great-grandfather Karl Ernst was clergyman to the last kings of Hanover, but when Hanover was conquered by the Prussians in 1866, he sent his seven sons out of Germany to keep them out of the army. All but one came to America, which is how my maternal grandfather got to New York, where he became a lawyer.

At the other end of the social scale, in *Daddy King*, Reverend Martin Luther King, Sr., discussed his family:

My parents were poor farming people, sharecroppers working the land around Stockbridge, Georgia, when I was born there on the nineteenth of December 1899.

My father, James Albert King, was a lean, tough little fellow very wiry and strong. As a young man, he'd worked in a rock quarry near town, but lost part of his right hand in an explosion one day. He became quite bitter about this in later years. Quarry work paid fairly good money in those days, more than any Negro was ever going to make farming someone else's land.

My mother, Delia Lindsay, met my father a short while after his accident. They were married there in Stockbridge, and because she was from farming people and was never afraid of work a day in her life, the two of them decided to set up housekeeping and work some acres of cotton for a local landowner.

As time went along and my daddy took to drinking a lot of whiskey, as he came to have a look of very quiet but very serious fire in his eyes, more and more people just left him alone, too. My mother was a different kind of person. She had a temper, too, maybe even worse than Papa's in some ways, because it was so deep in her that anything bringing it out was bringing out some real trouble. But Mama was at peace with herself because of her abiding faith.

By telling the little he knew about his family, Frederick

Douglass describes the hardship of slavery. He wrote:

My mother was named Harriet Bailey. She was the daughter of Isaac and Betsey Bailey, both colored, and quite dark. My mother was of a darker complexion than either my grandmother or grandfather.

My father was a white man. He was admitted to be such by all I ever heard speak of any parentage. The opinion was also whispered that my master was my father, but of the correctness of this opinion, I know nothing; the means of knowing was withheld from me.

My mother and I were separated when I was but an infant, before I knew her as my mother. It is a common custom, in the part of Maryland from which I ran away, to part children from their mother at a very early age. Frequently, before the child has reached its twelfth month, its mother is taken from it, and hired out on some farm a considerable distance off, and the child is placed under the care of an older woman, too old for field labor.

In writing about his family, H.L. Mencken included this amusing incident involving a favorite relative:

My brother Charlie and I were very fond of Aunt Pauline, who was immensely hospitable, and the best doughnut cook in all Baltimore. When the creative urge seized her, which was pretty often, she would make enough doughnuts to fill a large tin wash-boiler, and then send word down to Hollins Street that there was a surprise waiting in Fayette Street.

It was uphill all the way, but Charlie and I always took it on the run, holding hands and pretending that we were miraculously dashing carhorses. After Charlie had got down his first half dozen doughnuts and was taking time out to catch his breath and scrape the grease and sugar off his face, Aunt Pauline would ask, "How do they taste?" And he would always answer, "They taste like more."

In recording your ancestors, include those who might not have been pillars in the community. Don't attempt to patch over cracks in the foundation. In most family tribes there is at least one character that the others would like to forget.

I had a distant cousin who stole anything that wasn't tied down. If his folks hadn't covered his thefts, he would have been jailed at an early age. When he was thirty, he stole another man's wife and took off for California, never to be heard from again.

When doing a "roots trip" to County Cork, I discovered that in Ireland a relative's reputation has a long life.

At Kilronan House, the family homestead, I met Patrick Crowley, the current owner who had lived there since his birth. He was a sturdy farmer with a cheerful red face. His grandfather had bought the place from a Jagoe, When Patrick asked me about my history with Kilronan House, I told him that in 1758 when he married a Catholic, my ancestor had been disowned by his irate father.

"Ah, yes," Patrick said thoughtfully. "I've heard he was a very rough man."

6

First Home

Mansion or hut, your first home was your whole world within reach. This place was the stage for your early formation where you initiated awareness. Throughout your life, it will occasionally reappear in your dreams.

In this surrounding, you coasted through those early days filled with discovery and new associations. As it was an important part of your being, in writing your story you should consider including a description of your first home.

It was a unique place because it changed in size. When you were little, your home seemed enormous. Every room was spacious, and the ceilings were sky-high. Then, when you returned as an adult, you found that everything had shrunk.

When I wrote my autobiography, I gave considerable importance to my childhood place in Gulfport, Mississippi. I devoted a chapter to describe the house and the yard. Then I wrote about the neighbors on either side.

Your first home was your whole world within reach.

Many of the things I described had a story attached. For example, the rose garden was where my father, on the advice of his bootlegger, buried a keg of bourbon. This seasoning technique wasn't successful because water seeped in. Father ended up with some funny tasting whiskey.

Inside the house, the stairway reminded me of the time Sammy, my pet opossum, caused a commotion. During a dinner party, Sammy got out of his box up in my room and ambled down the stairs. Everyone mistook him for a big rat.

The fireplace was the focal point of our living room. On cold winter evenings I used to sit there, staring into the red and blue flames, listening while we read out loud. It took us two months to get through *Gone with the Wind*.

In his memoirs, astronaut John Glenn did a thorough job in describing his early home. He wrote:

> We lived in a big house. When Mother and Dad decided to move to New Concord, they thought they could help pay for the house by renting rooms to college students. Dad had it built with four large rooms upstairs and installed the plumbing and coal-burning furnace himself. We always had upstairs boarders, even after the college decided that all the students should live on campus.
>
> Our house was on a gravel road called Shadyside Terrace. It sat high on an embankment overlooking the National Road, U.S. Route 40, at the western edge of town. Route 40 was the main road from Baltimore to St. Louis, and it followed the route of the old pioneer trail called the Zane Trace.

The downstairs of the house had a living room and dining room across the front. The kitchen and two bedrooms, including the one my parents shared, were in the back. My favorite room was the kitchen.

Mother was a good cook. She made a wonderful ham loaf, delicious corn mush, and savory pies and cakes. We ate there at a big table, where it was always warm and full of the smells of cooking. It was Dad's favorite room, too.

When you remember that Helen Keller was a little girl, both deaf and blind, it is interesting to read her description of her childhood home:

It is the custom in the South to build a small house near the homestead as an annex to be used on occasion. Such a house my father built after the Civil War, and when he married my mother they went to live in it. It was completely covered with vines, climbing roses and honeysuckles.

The Keller homestead, where the family lived, was a few steps away from our little rose-bower. It was called 'Ivy Green' because the house and the surrounding trees and fences were covered with beautiful English ivy. Its old-fashioned garden was the paradise of my childhood.

Even in the dark before my teacher came, I used to feel along the square stiff boxwood hedges, and guided by the sense of smell, would find the first violets and lilies. There, too, after a fit of temper, I went to find comfort and to hide my hot face in the cool leaves and grass.

Fidel Castro goes to such detail in describing where he grew up that you can practically hear the chickens cackling under the house. This is his account:

> There was the family home and an annex containing a few small offices that had been built on one corner. Its architecture could be described as Spanish. It was because my father was a Spaniard from Galicia. In the villages there they had the custom of working a plot of land and keeping the animals under the house during the winter or throughout the year. They raised pigs and kept some cows there.
>
> That's why I said my house was based on Galician architecture, because it was built on stilts. Between the dining room and the kitchen there was a flight of stairs leading down to the ground.
>
> The pit for cockfights was around 100 meters from the house, on the main road. During the sugar harvest, cockfights were held there every Sunday, also on December 25, around New Year's and every holiday.

During her miserable childhood, Isadora Duncan had no one place to remember as her first home. In telling her story, she wrote:

> When I was five we had a cottage on 23rd Street (in San Francisco). Failing to pay the rent, we could not remain there but moved to 17th Street, and in a short time, as funds were low, the landlord objected, so we moved to 22nd Street, where

we were not allowed to live peacefully but were moved to 10th Street.

The history continued in this way, with an indefinite number of removals. When I rose to read it to the school, the teacher became very angry. She thought I was playing a bad joke, and I was sent to the principal, who sent for my mother. When my poor mother read the paper she burst into tears and vowed that it was only too true. Such was our nomadic existence.

If you don't want to write about your first home, you might tell of any other early residence you consider worth recording. To emphasize their poverty, Charlie Chaplin described in detail his teenage home:

And I would return to a row of old derelict houses that sat back off the Kennington Road, to 3 Pownall Terrace, and mount the rickety stairs that led to our small garret.

The house was depressing and the air was foul with stale slop and old clothes, The room was stifling, a little over twelve feet square and seemed smaller and the slanting ceiling seemed lower. The table against the wall was crowded with dirty plates and tea cups and in the corner, snug against the lower wall, was an old iron bed which Mother had painted white.

Between the bed and the window was a small fire-grate, and at the foot of the bed an old armchair that unfolded and became a single bed upon which my brother Sydney slept. But now, Sydney was away at sea.

When you paint with words the picture of your first home, be lavish in recalling your associations and sensations. Consider how this place and its geographic location might have affected your life. Had it been otherwise, you might be a different person.

7

Early Years

Following infancy, your next fifteen years was an interesting period of formation. It was the span when your childhood blended into adolescence, then stumbled ahead to the beginning of your adult life. During this time, you began to recognize your uniqueness.

In recording this era, you have to try and see it through the eyes of the kid you once were. In doing this, you want neither to denounce reality nor to be bound by it. There's a happy middle between the literal and the absurd—between the absolute and the fanciful.

Reality is a good medium to work with, but it can be a good idea occasionally to make it more enjoyable. You are writing your memoirs about what you want to be remembered, whether or not it's true. The mind becomes what it perceives and memory is flexible. So, don't hesitate to test the elasticity of truth in order to make a good story.

I did this when I wrote about Nelson Eddy having dinner at our house. At that

During this time, you began to recognize your uniqueness.

47

time I was thirteen and the future Hollywood idol was a young baritone making a concert tour throughout the south. As Mother's committee had arranged for his coming to town, she invited him to dinner.

He was so handsome that our cook wanted to show him off to Amanda, who was our neighbor's cook. During the meal, I was surprised to see Amanda coming in from the kitchen carrying the bread. As she served the table, she was so busy eyeing Nelson Eddy that she dumped all the hot biscuits in my lap. The part about her dropping the biscuits is embellished truth. This could have happened and it makes a good story.

In writing about your life, you need to demonstrate a clear vision of childhood. In 440, when St. Patrick wrote his autobiography, he sloughed off information about his childhood that must have been interesting. He only wrote:

> As a youth, nay, almost as a boy not able to speak, I was taken captive, before I knew what to pursue and what to avoid.

In describing their childhood, two authors told of their impressions during this period. In *An Hour before Daylight,* Jimmy Carter wrote:

> My most persistent impression as a farm boy was of the earth. There was closeness, almost an immersion, in the sand, loam and red clay that seemed natural, and constant.

> The soil caressed my bare feet, and the dust was always boiling up from the dirt road that passed fifty feet from our front door; so that inside our

clapboard house, the red clay particles, ranging in size from face powder to grits, were ever present, particularly in the summertime, when the wooden doors were kept open, and the screens just stopped the trash and some of the less adventurous flies.

In his autobiography from an earlier era and from a different part of the country, Henry Adams told of his youth (written in the third person):

Boys are wild animals, rich in the treasures of sense, but the New England boy had a wider range of emotions than boys of more equable climates. He felt his nature crudely, as it was meant.

To the boy Henry Adams summer was drunken. Among senses, smell was the strongest—smell of hot pine-woods and sweet fern in the scorching summer noon; of new-mowed hay; of ploughed earth; of box hedges; of peaches, lilacs, syringas; of stables, barns, cow-yards; of salt water and low tide on the marshes, nothing came amiss.

Next to smell came taste, and the children knew the taste of everything they saw or touched, from pennyroyal and flagroot to the shell of a pignut and the letters of a spelling book—the taste of A-B, AB suddenly revived on the boy's tongue sixty years afterwards. Light, line and color as sensual pleasures, came later and were as crude as the rest. The New England light is glare, and the atmosphere harshens color.

The boy was a full man before he even knew
what was meant by atmosphere; his idea of pleasure in light was the glaze of a New England
sun. His idea of color was a peony, with the dew
of each morning on its petals. The intense blue
of the sea, as he saw it a mile or two away, from
the Quincy hills, the cumuli in a June afternoon
sky, the strong reds and greens and purples of
colored prints and children's picture-books, as
the American colors that ran; these were ideals.
The opposites or antipathies, were the cold grays
of November evenings and the thick muddy thaws
of Boston winter. With such standards, the
Bostonian could not but develop a double nature. Life was a double thing. After a January
blizzard, the boy who could look with pleasure
into the violent snow-glare of the cold white sun-
shine, with its intense lights and shade, scarcely
knew what was meant by tone.

In his memoir *Colored People,* Henry Louis Gates,
Jr., clearly recalled the discrimination he and his family
endured in West Virginia during the 1960s:

> For most of my childhood, we couldn't eat in res-
> taurants or sleep in hotels, we couldn't use
> certain bathrooms or try on clothes in stores.
> Mama insisted that we dress up when we went
> to shop. She was a fashion plate when she went
> to clothing stores, and wore white pads called
> shields under her arms so her dress or blouse
> would show no sweat.
>   "We'd like to try this one," she'd say carefully,

articulating her words precisely and properly. "We don't buy clothes we can't try on," she'd say when they declined, as we'd walk—in Mama's dignified manner—out of the store.

It's interesting to read about Charlie Chaplin's childhood stunt in creating a role that later would make him famous. When he was eight years old, his father arranged for him to join a dancing troupe. In his autobiography, he wrote:

> After practicing six weeks I was eligible to dance with the troupe. But now that I was past eight years old, I had lost my assurance, and confronting the audience for the first time gave me stage fright. I could hardly move my legs. It was weeks before I could solo dance as the rest of them did.
>
> I was not particularly enamored of being just a clog dancer in a troupe of eight lads. Like the rest of them, I was ambitious to do a single act, not only because it meant more money but also because I instinctively felt it would be more gratifying than just dancing. I would have liked to be a boy comedian—but that would have required nerve, to stand on the stage alone.
>
> Nevertheless, my first impulse to do something other than dance was to be funny. My ideal was a double act, two boys dressed as comedy clowns. I told it to one of the other boys, and we decided to become partners.
>
> It became our cherished dream. We would call ourselves "Bristol and Chaplin the Millionaire

Tramps," and would wear whiskers and big dia-
mond rings. It embraced every aspect of what
we thought would be funny and profitable, but,
alas, it never materialized.

In writing about his life in *The Man Who Listens to
Horses*, Roberts, one of the greatest horse trainers of all
time, told how he began discovering the language of
horses:

> It all dates from those summers alone in the high
> desert lying on my belly and watching wild horses
> with my binoculars for hours at a time. Straining
> to see in the moonlight, striving to fathom mus-
> tang ways, I knew instinctively I had chanced
> upon something important but could not know
> that it would shape my life. In 1948 I was a boy
> of thirteen learning the language of horses.
> In the wilderness of Nevada, the soil is silky
> and cool to the touch at dawn, and at midday will
> burn your skin. My summer vigils were marked
> off by the heat of the day and the cold of the
> night and a profound sense of solitude. It felt right
> to be under those vast skies on the dove-gray
> moonscape in the company of wild and wary
> horses. It was the mustangs who taught me their
> silent body grammar.

Like Monty Roberts, Mohandas Gandhi had good reason to remember his thirteenth year. He wrote:

> It is my painful duty to record here my marriage
> at the age of thirteen. As I see the youngsters of

the same age about me who are under my care and think of my own marriage, I am inclined to pity myself and to congratulate them on having escaped my lot. I can see no moral argument in support of such a preposterously early marriage.

My father put on a brave face in spite of his injuries, and took full part in the wedding. As I think of it, I can even today call before my mind's eye the place where he sat as he went through the different details of the ceremony. Little did I dream then that one day I should severely criticize my father for having married me as a child.

Everything on that day seemed to me right and proper and pleasing. There was also my own eagerness to get married. And as everything that my father did then struck me as beyond reproach, the recollection of those things is fresh in my memory. I can picture to myself, even today, how we sat on our wedding dais, how we performed The *Saptapadi,* how we, The newly wedded husband and wife, put The sweet *Kansar* into each other's mouth, and how we began to live together.

And oh! that first night. Two innocent children all unwittingly hurled themselves into The ocean of life. My brother's wife thoroughly coached me about my behaviour on The first night. I do not know who had coached my wife. I have never asked her about it, nor am I inclined to do so now.

The reader may be sure that we were too nervous to face each other. We were certainly too shy. How was I to talk to her, and what was I to say? The coaching could not carry me far. But no coaching is really necessary in such matters.

As you look back at where you have been, enjoy re-living these early years. Savor these young impressions and experiences that seemed so important. In fact, they were.

8

Grown Up

When concerned adults would recommend a change in my youthful behavior, they would begin with, "Now that you're grown up." I knew what to expect. Being "grown up" implied many things, such as:

"You're not a kid any more, so cut out the kid stuff."

"You've got to take on more responsibility."

"For heaven's sake, act your age."

We found that teenage can be a mean age—the link between the young years and adulthood. It was the time when you had no choice; you had to grow up. It was also an experience filled with memories worth recording.

If you have college days to recall, it was probably an exciting period because of many changes. That's especially true about the freshman year. In my case, during my first year in college I made friends, I enjoyed a different way of life, and I was in a part of the country that was completely foreign to me. In *Southern Boy,* I wrote:

I liked everything about Harvard

You're not a kid any more, so cut out the kid stuff.

55

except academia. The first thing that grabbed me when I arrived at Cambridge was the sense of tradition.

I had grown up in Gulfport, Mississippi, a new town that was only eighty years old. Now, I was standing in front of the statue of John Harvard, who had been anxiously waiting 300 years for my arrival.

During the fifth century, St. Augustine began his studies at the university of Carthage. He recorded that:

> The prestigious course of studies I was following looked as its goal to the law-courts, in which I was destined to excel and where I would earn a reputation all the higher in the measure that my performance was the more unscrupulous.
>
> Still young and immature, I began in the company of these people (corrupting upperclassmen) to study treatises on eloquence. This was a discipline in which I longed to excel, though my motive was the damnably proud desire to gratify my human vanity.
>
> In the customary course of study I had discovered a book author called Cicero, whose language is almost universally admired, though not its inner spring. This book of his is called *The Hortensius* and contains an exhortation to philosophy. This book changed my way of feeling.

In a speedy summation of his life, Jimmy Buffett, the noted singer and songwriter, squeezed in a lot of living after he started college. He wrote:

In four hundred words or less, this is what happened from adolescence until now: I made it
through adolescence without killing myself in a
car. I flunked out of college. I learned to play the
guitar, lived on the beach, lived in the French
Quarter, finally got laid, and didn't go to Vietnam.
I got back into school, started a band, got a job
on Bourbon Street, graduated from college,
flunked my draft physical, broke up my band, and
went out on the road solo, signed a record deal,
got married, moved to Nashville, had my guitar
stolen, bought a Mercedes, worked at *Billboard*
magazine, put out my first album, went broke,
wrecked the Mercedes, got divorced, and moved
to Key West.

In their autobiographies, both General Grant and
Dwight D. Eisenhower told about their preparation for going to West Point. General Grant wrote:

In the winter of 1838–9, I was attending school
at Ripley, only ten miles distant from Georgetown,
but spent the Christmas holidays at home.
    During this vacation my father received a let-
ter from the Honorable Thomas Morris, then
United States Senator from Ohio. When he read
it he said to me, "Ulysses, I believe you are going to receive the appointment."
    "What appointment?" I inquired.
    "To West Point, I have applied for it."
    "But I won't go," I said. He said he thought I
would, and I thought so too, if he did. I really had
no objection to going to West Point, except that I

had a very exalted idea of the acquirements necessary to get through.

I did not believe I possessed them, and could
not bear the idea of failure. There had been four
boys from our village, or its immediate neighbor-
hood, who had graduated from West Point, and
never a failure of anyone appointed from
Georgetown, except in the case of the one whose
place I was to take.

In 1911, after Eisenhower received his appointment
he had to report first to take an examination at Jefferson
Barracks outside of St. Louis, Missouri. He told about this
experience:

One night, while quartered there for the examination, I left the Barracks with another applicant,
and we wandered around the city. We walked
the streets for a time. Thinking we'd see more of
the city, we took a streetcar and, riding it to the
end of the line, found ourselves at a car barn in
East St. Louis, on the southern side of the Mississippi River. Now we had a problem.

No more streetcars were running. We saw no
sign of any other kind of transportation, and we
were lost. A heavy fog lay over the city, and we
could not orient ourselves by the stars. We did
think that by following the tracks backward we
would reach the river. This ruse failed when we
came to a point where the line branched, and
we had no idea which one to take.

Fortunately, in a nearby building, we saw a
dim light. There we hoped to find a friendly soul
who would set us on the right road to the city.

We knocked on the door, and soon heard some-one in the room moving towards us. The door, which was massive, began to open slowly, and the first thing we saw was the muzzle of a re-volver.

A voice said, "Who are you?"

We stammered that we just wanted help in getting back across the river. The man, who proved to be a bartender, apparently decided we were harmless young fellows, and he let us in, lowered the revolver, and gave us explicit instruc-tions.

We were within a block of the bridge. We crossed it at double-time, hoping to catch the final car for the Barracks, which we had been told left at 1:00 AM. We made it, but had the prob-lem of avoiding discovery upon reaching the Barracks.

At the main gate, a guard would have taken our names. We decided to avoid it. Instead we went down along the wall through the darkness, under the trees, to find a spot where we would be undetected as we scaled the wall. We got into our beds and lay there breathing heavily.

Then my friend said, "You know, when I looked down the barrel of that big pistol, I could see the whole funeral procession."

When he was in college, Abba Eban continued his participation in the Zionist movement. He wrote:

My Cambridge years were not occupied by Middle Eastern cultures alone. There was intense development in my Zionist vocation. I became president of the university synagogue, the Jewish Society and the Zionist Group. Although Palestine was not the central issue of preoccupation in a world darkened by Franco, Mussolini and Hitler, there were ample opportunities for me to defend my cause against its Arab and British opponents. By the time I left the university in my early twenties, I had contributed to most English language Zionist journals and had written articles and letters in the *New Statesman* and *Spectator.* The Zionist office in London occasionally mobilized me for speeches within the university communities and beyond.

In the Story of My Life, Helen Keller tells about her determination to go to college:

In October 1896, I entered the Cambridge School for Young Ladies, to be prepared for Radcliffe.
     When I was a little girl, I visited Wellesley and surprised friends by the announcement, "Some day I shall go to college––but I shall go to Harvard." When asked why I would not go to Wellesley, I replied that there were only girls there.
     The thought of going to college took root in my head and became an earnest desire, which impelled me to enter into competition for a degree with seeing and hearing girls, in the face of the strong opposition of many true and wise friends. When I left New York the idea had become a fixed purpose, and it was decided that I should go to Cambridge. That was the nearest

approach I could get to Harvard and to the fulfill-
ment of my childish declaration.

Billy Graham gives this amusing account of his days
at Wheaton College near Chicago:

When I talked at my customary rapid clip, people
looked at me curiously, as if my heavily accented
drawl were a foreign language. At six-foot-two, I
was too tall to fade into the background. When I
went out for the wrestling team, probably at about
the 160-pound class, I looked like a python on
the mat. Two defeats in intercollegiate matches
ended that career.

At twenty-one years of age, I was older than
most of my mates, which did not help my self-
image. I was sure they were staring at my Li'l
Abner appearance, what with out-of-style clothes
and brogan shoes. I decided to do something
about it.

One day, tagging along with some other students, I went to Chicago's Maxwell Street, a kind
of open-air flea market. On Monday morning, if
you were the first there and a sharp bargainer,
you could talk the merchant down to about a third
of the asking price. For $4.95 I bought a beauti-
ful turquoise tweed suit and wore it proudly to a
football game in October. Then it started to rain.
The pants legs shrank up my ankles, and the
seat of the pants became so tight that I burst the
seam. I couldn't get home fast enough!

When you are recording your "grown up" days, you

may find many things to include. In the autumn of life, it is a pleasure to look back on the days of spring. Recalling this period of your life will invoke exciting memories that catch a glimpse of themselves.

9

Adult Life

Your early adult experiences affected the rest of your life. In remembering those days, you have such a large volume of information that it's difficult to select what to tell about. From the following examples, you'll find that others have chosen from a wide variety of happenings. For instance, two men from antiquity implied that adult life and adultery are synonymous. In 1100, Peter Abela wrote about his manhood romance:

> Now there dwelt in that same city of Paris a certain young girl named Heloise, the niece of a canon who was called Fulbert. Her uncle's love for her was equaled only by his desire that she should have the best education which he could possibly procure for her.
>
> Of no mean beauty, she stood out above all by reason of her abundant knowledge of letters. Now this virtue

You have such a large volume of information that it's difficult to select what to tell about.

is rare among women, and for that very reason it doubly graced the maiden, and made her the most worthy of renown in the entire kingdom.

Abelard then persuaded the uncle to let him move into the house to tutor the beautiful Heloise. He continued in his memoir:

> We were united first in the dwelling that sheltered our love, and then in the hearts that burned with it. Under the pretext of study we spent our hours in the happiness of love, and learning held out to us the secret opportunities that our passion craved. Our speech was more of love than of the books, which lay open before us.
>
> It was not long after this that Heloise found that she was pregnant, and of this she wrote to me in the utmost exultation, at the same time asking me to consider what had best be done.

When St. Augustine was between nineteen and twenty-eight years old, he was both teaching law and enjoying a relationship with his significant other. In telling about this period, he wrote:

> During these years, I was teaching the art of rhetoric, selling talkative skills apt to sway others because greed swayed me. Yet I preferred to have good pupils, or such as passed for good, and without any trickery on my part I taught them the tricks of the trade, never such as would secure the condemnation of the innocent, though sometime such as were calculated to get the guilty acquitted.

At this time I lived with a girl not bound to me in lawful wedlock but sought out by the roving eye of reckless desire; all the same she was the only girl I had, and I was sexually faithful to her. This experience taught me at first hand what a difference there is between a marriage contracted for the purpose of founding a family, and a relationship of love charged with carnal desire.

Jane Goodall wrote about her first trip to Africa, which determined her future:

On Wednesday morning, December 18, 1956, I received a letter from Marie Claude Mange. Clo, as she was known, had been my best friend at school. I hadn't heard from her for a while and was surprised when I saw that her letter was from Africa.

I still remember the Kenyan stamps—there was an elephant on one and two giraffes on the other. Her parents, she wrote, had just bought a farm in Kenya. Would I like to join them for a visit? Would I ever!

While visiting her friends in Kenya, she had this opportunity:

It began after a dinner party when I was being given a lift back to my quarters. "If you are interested in animals," someone said, "you should meet Louis Leakey."

So I made an appointment and went to see the famous paleontologist and anthropologist at the Caryndon Museum of Natural History.

After his interview, Dr. Leakey immediately hired Jane as his personal secretary.

John Glenn, the first man to orbit the earth in space, told about his plans in early 1958 to get into the astronaut program:

> Without really knowing it, I was seeing the very beginning of the U.S. manned space flight program. At that stage, however, it consisted of research and rumors. If there had been a call for a volunteer, I would have been at the front of the line. But the Eisenhower administration had not publicly committed itself to sending a person into space.

In late summer of that year President Eisenhower signed the National Aeronautics and Space Act into law. Realizing that there would be a call for volunteers, John Glenn began to prepare, including dropping his weight from 208 pounds down to 178. NASA screened the records of 508 test pilots and eliminated four-fifths of the prospects:

> Early in 1959 I received orders stamped "top secret," directing me to report for a briefing at the Pentagon, where I found myself in a room full of test pilots. A pair of NASA officials confirmed the rumor that had been circulated at Bureau. Abe Silverstein and George Low said NASA needed volunteers for its program to send men into suborbital and orbital flight. These men would be called astronauts.
>
> It would require a new kind of test flying that had never been done, but it was a necessary

step in the space race with the Soviets. Anybody who volunteered could reconsider his choice at any time, they said. I volunteered without hesitation.

In 1740, the English actor Colley Libber wrote in his autobiography about the first appearance of actresses:

The other advantage I was speaking of is that before the Restoration (the reign of King Charles II) no actresses had ever been seen upon the English stage.

The characters of women on former theatres were perform'd by boys, or young men of the most effeminate aspect. And what grace or masterstroke of action can we conceive such hoydens to have been capable of? This defect was so well consider'd by Shakespeare, that in few of his plays, he has any greater dependence upon the ladies, than in the innocence and simplicity of a Desdemona, an Ophelia, or in the short specimen of a fond and virtuous Portia.

The additional objects then of real, beautiful women could not but draw a proportion of new admirers to the theatre. We may imagine too, that these actresses were not ill chosen, when it is well known that more than one of them had charms sufficient at their leisure hours to calm and mollify the cares of empire.

As a young ambitious architect, Frank Lloyd Wright told about getting a job where he worked with the prominent firm of Adler and Sullivan:

Thus began an association lasting nearly seven years. Mr. Sullivan had been interested and interesting. His drawings a delight to work upon and work out. His manner toward me markedly different from his manner toward the other men. Mark me it might, and mark me it did. I soon found my place in the office had to be fought for.

The work was going well. I could do it. The master was pleased. This evident favoritism of the master together with my own natural tendency to mind my own business, coupled with a distaste for most of the Adler and Sullivan men, had, in the course of a few weeks, set them against me.

I was unpopular from the first day. And I was baited in various ways. My hair of course. My dress a bit too individual, I suppose. There would be casual conversation behind me with unmistakable reference to me. Studied interference with my work. The gang had evidently combined to "get me."

General Colin Powell gave a moving account related to his tour of duty in Vietnam:

Life at Duc Pho took crazy pendulum swings from the trite to the heartbreaking. One afternoon I was getting Coke and beer helicopters out to the firebases—a daily priority the exec dared not miss—when Colonel Lowder sent word that he had run into a stiff fight at Firebase Liz and needed help.

I ordered up a "slick," a bare-bone UH-I helicopter, no seats, just space and a couple of door guns, had it loaded with 5.56mm rifles and 7.6 machine gun ammunition, and headed out over the treetops. We landed at Liz near dusk and quickly unloaded.

A grim-faced Lowder told me to take back nine of our casualties. The vulnerability of a helicopter on the ground left little time for niceties. The nine KHAs [killed by hostile actions, the Army's replacement term for KIA, killed in action] were rolled into ponchos and loaded onto the slick. As we took off in the half-light, I slumped to the floor, facing nine recently healthy young American boys, now stacked like cordwood.

People in combat develop a protective numbness that allows them to go on. That night I saw this shield crack. Eventually, the bodies were taken from the slick into the field hospital to be confirmed as dead. Medical staffers unrolled each poncho and examined the bodies with brisk efficiency, until the last one.

I heard a nurse gasp, "Oh my God, it's . . ." The final casualty was a young medic from their unit who had volunteered to go out to the firebase the day before. Nurses and medics started crying. I turned and left them to their duty.

In your courageous adventure into the past, it's good not to be evasive about including your casualties and failures. They, too, were learning experiences. The person who has never failed is one who has never taken a chance, and telling of unsuccessful ventures gives your autobiography the charm of honesty. Your story proves you have not failed to live an experimental life. As a female entrepreneur in the fourteenth century, Margery Kempe wrote, in the third person, about her disastrous venture in the brewery business:

> And then, for pure covetise and for to maintain her pride, she gan to brew and was one of the greatest brewers in the town, a three year or four till she lost much good, for she had never ure thereto.
>
> For though she had never so good servants and cunning in brewing, yet it would never prove with them. For when the ale was as fair standing under barm and any man might see, suddenly the barm would fall down that all the ale was lost brewing after other, that her servants were ashamed and not dwell with her.
>
> Then this creature thought how God had punished her before time, and she could not beware, and now eftsoons by losing her goods, and then she left and brewed no more.

In 1876, when Anthony Trollope wrote his autobiography at age sixty-one, he included this failure from his early career:

> When I had been married a year my first novel was finished. In July 1845 I took it with me to the north of England, and entrusted the MS. to my mother to do with it the best she could with the publishers in London. No one had read it but my wife nor, as far as I am aware, has any other friend of mine ever read a word of my writing before it was published.
>
> My mother, however, did the best she could

for me, and soon reported that Mr. Newby of Mortimer Street was to publish the book. It was to be printed at his expense and he was to give me half the profits. Half the profits!

Many a young author expects much from such an undertaking. I can with truth declare that I expected nothing. And I got nothing. Nor did I expect fame, or even acknowledgment. I was sure that the book would fail, and it did fail most absolutely.

In choosing the events of your adult life to include in your autobiography, test each one by determining if it has the need to be documented. Something qualifies if it has historic interest, has special value, or is entertaining. Don't be like my aged cousin Slatter who used to begin one of his many stories with, "I don't want to bore you, but I want to tell you. . . ." Believe me, he did both.

10

Special People

The things you do, think, and say have echoes from those who have nudged you along the way. Even if these submerged directives are faint, they are real. It's good to acknowledge their source. By including these special men and women in your autobiography, you perpetuate their memory.

These influential persons might have been your parents, relatives, teachers, associates, mentors, or friends. Each has made a valuable contribution. The more important of these merit being included in the story of your life because they had an impact on your consciousness.

Sir Laurence Olivier, Cardinal Newman, and Helen Keller paid special tribute to their mentors. In 1927, when Olivier auditioned, at age seventeen, for a scholarship in a school for speech and dramatics, he was judged by a very perceptive woman. This is his description:

Elsie Fogerty was not a tall woman, and she possessed the slight thickness of set to be expected in late

You perpetuate their memory.

middle age. She was smartly dressed with a carefully chosen hat; dark-haired with some assistance; her head was arresting, even distinguished, but not handsome or very attractive. . . .

When it was over I was beckoned down to sit with Miss Fogerty at her table. She obviously found my efforts commendable enough, because without any beating about the bush she informed me that the scholarship was mine. . . .

Before I left she gave me one unforgettable, very special word of advice, which has been imprinted forever in my memory. She now leant towards me and said, "You have weakness here," and placed the tip of her little finger on my forehead. . . .

I felt immediately the wisdom of this pronouncement. There was obviously some shyness behind my gaze. This was a thing I comprehended so completely that it shadowed my first few years as an actor. I am not imputing to Elsie Fogerty the responsibility for a psychological block, it was simply not like that; I knew it was true, there was a weakness there.

It lasted until I discovered the protective shelter of nose-putty and enjoyed a pleasurable sense of relief and realization when some character part called for a sculptural addition to my face, affording me the relief of an alien character and enabling me to avoid anything so embarrassing as self-representation.

In his autobiography, Cardinal Newman wrote this about a special teacher:

And now as to Dr. Whately, I owe him a great deal. He was a man of generous and warm heart. He was particularly loyal to his friends, and to use the common phrase, "all his geese were swans." While I was still awkward and timid in 1822, he took me by the hand, and acted the part to me of a gentle and encouraging instructor. He emphatically opened my mind and taught me to think and to use my reason. . . .

He had done his work towards me, or nearly so, when he had taught me to see, with my own eyes and to walk with my own feet.

In the dedication of her autobiography, Helen Keller paid tribute to her great friend and benefactor:

To Alexander Graham Bell, who taught the deaf to speak and enabled the listening ear to hear speech from the Atlantic to the Rockies, I dedicate this story of my life.

At an early age, Helen Keller first met Dr. Bell when her father took her to visit him in Washington. Here is her account of this first meeting:

Child as I was, I at once felt the tenderness and sympathy which endeared Dr. Bell to so many hearts, as his wonderful achievements enlist their admiration. He held me on his knee while I examined his watch, and he made it strike for me. He understood my signs, and I knew it and loved him at once.

But I did not dream that that interview would

be the door through which I should past from
darkness into light, from isolation to friendship,
companionship, knowledge, love. . . . Since then
I have spent many happy days with him at Washington and at his beautiful home in the heart of
Cape Breton Island, near Baddeck.

Here in Dr. Bell's laboratory, or in the field on
the shore of the great Bras d'Or, I have spent
many delightful hours listening to what he had to
tell me about his experiments, and helping him
fly kites by means of which he expects to discover the laws that shall govern the future airships.

Dr. Bell is proficient in many fields of science,
and has the art of making every subject he
touches interesting, even the most abstruse theo-
ries. He makes you feel that if you only had more
time, you, too, might be an inventor. He has a
humorous and poetic side, too.

His dominating passion is his love for children. He is never quite so happy as when he has
a little deaf child in his arms. His labours in be-
half of the deaf will live on and bless generations
of children yet to come; and we love him alike for
what he himself has achieved and for what he
has evoked from others.

Thomas Jefferson and Dwight Eisenhower included
accounts of other famous people. In the story of his life,
the third president wrote:

I left Monticello on the first of March 1799 for
New York. At Philadelphia I called on the vener-
able and beloved Franklin. He was then on the

bed of sickness from which he never rose.

My recent return from a country in which he had left so many friends, and the perilous convulsions to which they had been exposed, revived all his anxieties to know what part they had taken, what had been their course, and what their fate. He went over all in succession, with rapidity and animation almost too much for his strength.

When all his inquires were satisfied and a pause took place, I told him I had learnt with much pleasure that, since his return to America, he had been occupied in preparing for the world the history of his own life. I cannot say much of that, said he; but I will give you a sample of what I shall leave and he directed his little grandson (William Bache), who was standing by the bedside, to hand him a paper from the table to which he pointed. He did so; and the Doctor, putting it into my hands, desired me to take it and read it at my leisure. . . .

It contained a narrative of the negotiations between Dr. Franklin and the British Ministry, when he was endeavoring to prevent the contest of arms which followed. The negotiation was brought about by the intervention of Lord Howe and his sister, who I believe was called Lady Howe.

General Eisenhower recalled another prominent military man. He wrote:

General Pershing was not a colorful man and he had one deplorable habit; he was always late—

up to an hour or more—for every engagement. When no one else was available, I acted as temporary aide, and it was always difficult, indeed embarrassing, to try to explain to the host why we were so late. The General seemed to be oblivious to the passage of time and he made no excuse for the long hours of waiting he imposed on any prospective host.

In his later years, I visited General Pershing in his room at Walter Reed Hospital. He grew weaker and weaker and it became almost impossible to talk with him. But whenever he spoke from his hospital bed, it was always as a senior commander.

I had the impression he was standing stiffly erect, Sam Brown belt and all. He managed to convey how much he appreciated visits by younger officers. Before he had taken to his bed, the slim, straight figure was an imposing presence.

To all the veterans of World War I, he is the single hero, and they remember him with respect and admiration, even if not affection. He had the reputation of being something of a martinet, but at the same time he was knowledgeable and fair. I liked him, and we all owed him respect and admiration for the way he had carried responsibility in that war.

In his autobiography published after his death, Anthony Trollope paid this tribute to a fellow author:

On Christmas Day 1863 we were startled by the news of Thackeray's death. I had known him only for four years, but had grown into much intimacy with him and his family. I regard him as one of the most tenderhearted human beings I ever knew, who, with an exaggerated contempt for the foibles of the world at large, would entertain an almost equally exaggerated sympathy with the joys and troubles of individuals around him.

He had been unfortunate in early life—unfortunate in regard to money—unfortunate with an afflicted wife—unfortunate in having his home broken up before his children were fit to be his companions. This threw him too much upon clubs and taught him to dislike general society. But it never affected his heart, or clouded his imagination. He could still revel in the pangs and joys of fictitious life, and could still feel—as he did to the very last—the duty of showing to his readers the evil consequences of evil conduct.

In telling the story of his life, the modern author Stephen King expressed his appreciation for a very special member of his family. He wrote:

My wife made a crucial difference during those two years I spent teaching at Hampden (and washing sheets at New Franklin Laundry during the summer vacation). If she had suggested that the time I spent writing stories on the front porch of our rented house on Pond Street or in the laundry room of the rented trailer on Klatt Road in Hermond was wasted time, I think a lot of the heart would have gone out of me.

Tabby never voiced a single doubt, however.

Her support was a constant, one of the few good things I could take as a given. Whenever I see a first novel dedicated to a wife (or husband), I smile and think, *There's someone who knows.* Writing is a lonely job. Having someone who believes in you makes a lot of difference. They don't have to make speeches. Just believing is usually enough.

When recording an event during his career with the *Baltimore Evening Sun,* H. L. Mencken expressed his admiration for Walter W. Abell, the president and grandson of the founder of the newspaper. This incident occurred when Mencken was the Sunday editor. He let slip through a story from their Paris correspondent. As a result, the sensitive Baltimorians were shocked to read that prehistoric animals could fart. This is his account:

> I usually read his copy carefully, but one day I slipped, and so did the proof room, and the result was the appearance the next Sunday of an article describing the indelicate behavior of some prehistoric animals alleged to have been discovered in the interior of Alaska. It told how those of one species pursued those of another species, and how the pursued tried to throw off the pursuers by letting blasts *a posteriori.*

Walter was very grave, but also very polite. Not a word of upbraiding came out of him. Instead, he delivered himself a long and murky lecture on the duties and responsibilities of a copy-reader, laying heavy stress on carefulness. Inasmuch as I had done a hundred times as much copy-reading as he had, I needed no such instruction, but I received it as politely as it was given, and we parted on the best of terms. The matter was never mentioned again.

In the last chapter of her autobiography *Me: Stories of My Life,* Katharine Hepburn summarized those who helped her in her career. She listed twenty-six people, including her cook.

11

Humor

Since life is a long lesson in humility, sometimes it's healthy to poke fun at yourself. With rare exception, humor is missing in most autobiographies. This implies that we take ourselves too seriously.

It makes good reading to occasionally make yourself the object of laughter. Some of the humor I detected in autobiographies was unintended. For example, it's amusing to read of Margery Kempe, in the fourteenth century, documenting what she considered her virtue of chastity. In the third person, she wrote:

> It befell upon a Friday, on Midsummer Eve, in right hot weather, as this creature was coming from York, bearing a bottle with beer in her hand, and her husband a cake in his bosom, he asked his wife this question. "Margery, if there came a man with a sword and would smite off my head unless I should come kindly with you as I have done before, sayeth me truth of your conscience—

Sometimes it's healthy to poke fun at yourself.

for you say you will not lie—whether would you suffer my head to be smote off, or else suffer me to meddle with you again, as I did before?"

"Alas, sir," she said, "why move you this matter, when we have been chaste these eight weeks?"

"Because I will know the truth of your heart.

And then she said with great sorrow, "Forsooth, I had rather see you be slain than we should turn again to our uncleanness."

And he said, "You are no good wife."

There is hidden humor in Carl Jung's account of Sigmund Freud's unusual behavior. He wrote:

The year 1909 proved decisive for our relationship. In Bremen the much-discussed incident of Freud's fainting fit occurred.

It was provoked indirectly by my interest in the "peat-bog corpses." I knew that in certain districts of Northern Germany these so-called bog corpses were to be found. They are the bodies of prehistoric men who either drowned in the marshes or were buried there.

This interest of mine got on Freud's nerves. "Why are you so concerned with these corpses?" he asked me several times. He was inordinately vexed by the whole thing and during one such conversation, while we were having dinner together, he suddenly fainted.

Afterward he said to me that he was convinced that all this chatter about corpses meant I had death-wishes toward him. I was more than surprised by this interpretation. I was alarmed by the intensity of his fantasies so strong that obviously, they could cause him to faint.

If you heard this account without knowing the name of the person who fainted, you'd probably think this fellow needed a good psychoanalyst.

As another example of unintended humor, in his autobiography, written in 1666 with the boastful title of *Grace Abounding in the Chief of Sinners,* John Bunyan gave this account of his effort to save souls:

> There was a young man in our own town to whom my heart was knit more than to any other, but he being a most wicked creature for cursing and swearing and whoring, I now shook him off, and forsook his company.
>
> But about a quarter of a year after I had left him, I met him in a certain lane, and asked him how he did. He, after his old swearing and mad way, answered me with he was well. "But Harry," said I, "why do you swear and curse thus? What will become of you, if you die in this condition?"
>
> He answered me in a great chafe. "What would the devil do for company, if it were not for such as I am?"

Katharine Hepburn laughed at herself in recalling a theater experience when she was a student at Bryn Mawr. This is her account:

> I played the lead man in one play—*The Truth About Blayds,* by A. A. Milne. I played the juvenile. I had to wear a wig, covering my long hair. And a pair of pants, a bit tight in the seat.

It was a modern play. I remember one frightful moment when we were giving a performance of it at the Colony Club in New York. Somehow or other I managed to put my hand in my pants pocket and then to sit down. After a bit I tried to get my hand out of the pocket. Impossible. I tried several times. I got a bit confused and kept yanking. This turned out to be a splendid laugh.

In her autobiography, Margaret Thatcher told how she answered foolish questions. When people asked her how it felt to be a woman prime minister, she would reply, "I don't know. I've never experienced the alternative."

When General Grant was recounting the end of the Civil War, he included this delightful story about Abraham Lincoln:

The Confederate States had sent peace commissioners to negotiate an end to the war in late January 1865.

Right here I might relate an anecdote of Mr. Lincoln. It was on the occasion of his visit with me just after he had talked with the peace commissioners at Hampton Roads. After a little conversation, he asked me if I had seen the overcoat of (Alexander H.) Stephens. I replied that I had.

"Well," said he, "didn't you think it was the biggest shuck and the littlest ear that ever you did see?"

There is always great humor when a stage actor has trouble with the stage. Early in his career in 1925, Laurence

Olivier had a minor role as a callboy in a play at the Brighton Hippodrome. This is his account:

> I stepped on to the stage, which as I had guessed was pretty sizeable. My cue came and I started forward, the stagehand just touched me on the sleeve and pointed to the bottom of the door; it was my turn to wave someone impatiently away. I gave the canvas door a push and strode manfully through it.
>
> Of course I did a shattering trip over the sill, sailed through the air, and before I knew what was happening to me, I found my front teeth wedged firmly between a pink bulb and a blue one in the middle of the footlights. I was appearing before a very ample house, which means that an audience reaction of any kind makes a thunderously loud noise to one on the stage facing it. The particular reaction stunned me for a second or two by its volume.
>
> I scrambled to my feet dusting myself off, and stood a while blinking at the audience; then turned and blinked at Ruby Miller, who was pro enough not to have turned a hair. I looked back once pleadingly to the audience, but they were not to be robbed as easily as that of their biggest laugh for ages.

One of the most delightful stories was Henry Adams' account of his confrontation with his grandfather, John Quincy Adams. In the third person, he wrote:

> One day he was putting up a fight in refusing to

go to school. This took place at the bottom of the long staircase, which led up to the door of the President's library, when the door opened, and the old man slowly came down.

Putting on his hat, he took the boy's hand without a word and walked with him, paralyzed by awe, up the road to the town. After the first moments of consternation at this interference in a domestic dispute, the boy reflected that an old gentleman close to eighty would never trouble himself to walk near a mile on a hot summer morning over a shadeless road to take a boy to school, and that it would be strange if a lad imbued with the passion of freedom could not find a corner to dodge around, somewhere before reaching the school door.

Then and always, the boy insisted that this reasoning justified his apparent submission. But the old man did not stop, and the boy found himself seated inside the school, and obviously the center of curious if not malevolent criticism. Not till then did the President release his hand and depart.

During the World War I, Charlie Chaplin told about this experience. Like Laurence Olivier, he encountered a stage problem.

In 1918, America had launched two Liberty Bond drives, and now Mary Pickford, Douglas Fairbanks and I were requested to open officially the third Liberty Bond campaign in Washington.

In Washington we paraded through the streets

like potentates, arriving at the football field where we were to give our initial address. The speakers' platform was made of crude boards with flags and bunting around it. Among the representatives of the Army and Navy standing about was one tall, handsome young man who stood beside me, and we made conversation.

I told him that I had never spoken before and was very anxious about it. "There's nothing to be scared about," he said confidently. "Just give it to them from the shoulder, tell them to buy the Liberty Bonds, don't try to be funny."

Very soon I heard my introduction, so I bounded *onto* the platform in Fairbanksian style and without a pause let fly a verbal machine-gun barrage, hardly taking a breath. "The Germans are at your door! We've got to stop them! And we will stop them if you buy Liberty Bonds! Remember, *each* bond you buy will save a soldier's life—a mother's son!—will bring this war to an early victory!"

I spoke so rapidly and excitedly that I slipped off the platform, grabbing Marie Dressier and fell with her on top of my handsome young friend, who happened to be then the Assistant Secretary of the Navy, Franklin D. Roosevelt.

In his autobiography *Memoirs of an Amnesiac,* the noted pianist and entertainer Oscar Levant told of his first visit to the White House:

In 1947 President Truman took a fancy to me, and I was invited to a state dinner for the Supreme

Court—the first one given since before the war. June and I had been warned not to be late as White House etiquette demanded punctuality; consequently we arrived a half-hour early. A naval aide greeted us, escorted us to the cloakroom, then through the long portrait-lined corridors to the entrance of the East Room, drew himself erect and announced, "Mr. and Mrs. Oscar Levant." We walked into an empty room. We walked around wondering to whom we had been announced. Not for twenty minutes did the next guests arrive.

After dinner I was escorted to the piano by a naval aide who stood at arm's length with a gun. I thought if I make a mistake, I'll be shot.

In my autobiography *Southern Boy*, I recalled an amusing story about my poor bombing skill during World War II. This is the story:

While serving as bombardier on one of my early B-25 missions over northern Italy, I really messed up. When we reached the I.P. (initial point), it was standard procedure to sight the target (the railroad terminal at Prato) by using the extended vision knob on the Norden bombsight. Then, as we got closer, I was to turn off the extended vision knob and zero in on the target. But I goofed.

In my excitement, I forgot to disconnect the knob. Just as I was about to tell the pilot I was starting the bomb run, over the intercom I heard our flight engineer call, "Bombs away!" My heart sank. By accident, I had dropped our bombs a mile short of the target.

For the rest of the flight home, I felt horrible. I had risked the lives of my crewmembers for a loused-up mission. If they had voted whether or not to throw me out of the plane without a parachute, I would have voted in favor of doing it.

That night after dinner, when I was sitting dejected in my tent, an enlisted man came looking for me. "Lieutenant, sir," he said, "I had to come to congratulate you. I've been a gunner on over 40 missions, and I've never before seen such a beautiful bombing job as you done today."

While I had my mouth open, he continued, "Yes, sir, I saw the whole thing. You remember that there was a straight highway way down below us. And there was only two trucks on it—coming towards each other. Then, just as they met, WHAMBO! You knocked out both of them. Lieutenant Jagoe, that was the best damn precision bombing anybody ever did. And I gotta shake your hand!"

Then he said with emotion, "Sir, it's men like you what makes me proud of being an American."

12

Important Events and Life Passages

This might be difficult. In reviewing the past, you will have to sift through a multitude of experiences. Don't overlook the fact that a lot of living comes in and goes out by the back door. You want to select those experiences that are the most important and should be recorded. For example, Frank Lloyd Wright wrote about the extensive study in 1921 that went into his building the Imperial Hotel in Tokyo. Two years later when the worst earthquake in history hit Japan and the Imperial Hotel was the only structure still intact, the world paid tribute to his genius.

In her story, Isadora Duncan included the heart-rending account of the car carrying her two children that crashed off a bridge and plunged into the river. One day after an enjoyable lunch in a Paris restaurant with her children and Lohengrin, her millionaire lover and father of her son, she stayed on for an afternoon rehearsal. She asked the nurse to wait with the children, and in her memoirs, Isadora Duncan recorded the nurse's reply:

You want to select those experiences that are the most important and should be recorded.

She said, "No, Madame, I think we had better return. The little ones need rest."

Then I kissed them and said, "I will also return soon." And then, in leaving, little Deirdre put her lips against the glass window. I leaned forward and kissed the glass on the spot where her lips were at that moment. The cold glass gave me an uneasy impression.

(Later that afternoon while resting at home after the rehearsal) I was thus lazily eating sweets and smiling to myself, thinking, "Lohengrin has returned, all will be well," when there came to my ears a strange, unearthly cry.

I turned my head. Lohengrin was there, staggering like a drunken man. His knees gave way—he fell before me and from his lips came this word: "The children—the children—are dead!"

I remember a strange stillness came upon me, only in my throat. I felt a burning, as if I had swallowed some live coals. But I could not understand. I spoke to him very softly; I told him to calm himself; I told him it could not be true.

I saw everyone about me weeping, but I did not weep. On the contrary, I felt an immense desire to console everyone. Looking back it is difficult for me to understand my strange state of mind. Was it that I was really in a state of clairvoyance, and that I knew that death does not exist—that those two little cold images of wax were not my children, but merely their cast-off garments? That the souls of my children lived in radiance, but live forever?

In reviewing the highlights of his career, horse trainer Monty Roberts wrote this about his initial association with royalty:

One December evening in 1988, when I was fifty-three years old, my longtime friend and neighbor, John Bowles, called me. "Monty," he said, "guess what? The Queen of England wants to meet you." Her Majesty, he said, was intrigued by my claims of being able to communicate with horses.

Not long afterward, Sir John Miller came to the farm for a demonstration and was excited by what he saw. On the way back to the house, he listed particular dates during the following year— Her Majesty's itinerary. It began to sink in that he was fitting me into the royal schedule. Some weeks later, I received a formal letter of invitation from Buckingham Palace: in April 1989 I was to spend a week at Windsor Castle.

For some days I had pondered the proper salutation to use should I meet the Queen of England. And should I bow, or was a handshake the order of the day? Far from home, the guest of a foreign nation, I wanted to do the right thing. But the Queen made it easy for me by offering her hand.

I shook it and said, "Your Majesty," and let it go at that. She was quick to put me at ease. "Come, Mr. Roberts," she said, "and show me this lions' cage in the center of the riding hall. I want you to tell me about it."

We shared a genuine fascination with horses and it was a great pleasure to talk with her about them. As her support continued, my respect and feeling of warmth for her grew steadily.

As dean of American journalism, Walter Trohan described this event when he was a young reporter:

It was St. Valentine's Day, February 14, 1929. John Pastor, a young lad who had been collecting marriage licenses, births and similar vital statistics, was being given a trial as police reporter.

Johnny was on the phone stuttering with excitement. He reported five men were killed in a garage. Isaac Gershman, the city editor, wouldn't believe him, and turned Pastor over to me, but insisted that I write a bulletin that five men had been injured in a fight. So, I wrote the bulletin of which I am not proud: "Five men are reported to have been injured in a fight at 2022 North Clark Street."

A moment later Johnny was back on the line swearing by all that was holy it wasn't five men dead but six and one was on the way to the hospital dying, and all had been cut down by machinegun fire. Pastor bypassed the unbelieving desk and gave it to me. I pounded out a second and more accurate bulletin, flung it at Gershman, and announced I was on my way, without asking for approval.

As I went out the door, I turned to ask if I could take a cab, City Press being more cautious about expense accounts. "The Clark streetcar runs right past the door," Gershman said.

Even so, I was the first man on the scene of

carnage, being careful to avoid the lunging of the crazed police dog chained to one of the garage trucks. The most memorable remark of the day was that of Willie O'Rourke of the *Chicago Evening American*, who looked down at his feet after tracking around the garage and said, "I've got more brains on my feet than I have in my head."

Other staffers joined me in tracing the path of ambush and the story of the slaying of six members of the George (Bugs) Moran mob, rivals of the Al Capone gang. I topped off the St. Valentine's Day murders by attending an all-star performance of *Macbeth* in Chicago's Auditorium Theatre. After all, the massacre was no more than a fitting prelude to the ten violent deaths in *Macbeth*.

In his autobiography, Thomas Jefferson gave this detailed account of the struggle within the Continental Congress in 1775:

The committee for drawing the Declaration of Independence desired me to do it. It was accordingly done, and being approved by them, I reported it to the House on Friday, the *28th* of June. On Monday, the 15th of July the original motion was carried in the affirmative by the votes of N. Hampshire, Connecticut, Massachusetts, Rhode Island, N. Jersey, Maryland, Virginia, N. Carolina, & Georgia. S. Carolina and Pennsylvania voted against it. Delaware having but two members present, they were divided.

Two days later, it was again moved and S. Carolina concurred in voting for it. In the meantime a third member had come post from the Delaware counties and turned the vote of that colony in favour of the resolution. Members of a different sentiment attending that morning from Pennsylvania also, their vote was changed, so that the whole 12 colonies who were authorized to vote at all, gave their voices for it.

Elie Wiesel recalled the naivete of his Jewish community who refused to believe the story of Nazi brutality:

In 1941 more than a thousand "foreign" Jews—those unable to document their Hungarian citizenship—were expelled from Hungarian territory to Polish Galicia.

I remember going to the station to say goodbye. Everybody was there. We thought we would see them again someday, but only one managed to escape and this was Moshe the beadle. Dazed, madness in his eyes, he told a hair-raising story. Those expelled (they were not yet called deportees) had been slaughtered and burned naked in ditches near Kolomyya, Stanislav and Kamenets-Podolski.

He talked on and on about the brutality of the killers, the agony of dying children and the death of old people, but no one believed him.

The Germans are human beings, people said, even if the Nazis aren't. The more convincing Moshe the beadle tried to be, the less seriously he was taken. . . .

I liked him and often kept him company, but I, too, could not bring myself to believe him. I listened, staring into his feverish face as he described his torment, but my mind resisted. Galicia is not exactly the end of the world, I told myself. It's only a few hours from here. If what he's saying were true, we would have heard.

In writing about his life, Reverend Martin Luther King, Sr., gave a detailed account of his personal tragedy, which was to be of historic importance:

> I parked and Bunch (his wife) and I rushed into the church building. We went upstairs to my study without exchanging a word, and I turned on the radio next to my desk. M. L. (Martin Luther, Jr.) had been shot, an announcer was saying, and he's suffered a very serious wound.
>
> I turned to Bunch. She was calm, but the tears had started pouring down her face. No sound came, though. The crying was silent as we waited for more specific news. I began praying, filling the study with my words.
>
> Soon more news had been received by a local radio station that indicated M. L. was hurt but still alive. Another report came through, saying the bullet had struck him in the shoulder, and I heard myself asking, "Lord, let him live, let him be alive!"
>
> But moments later the newscaster had a final, sober bulletin: Martin Luther King, Jr., had been shot to death while standing on the balcony of the Lorraine Motel in Memphis. Again, I turned to Bunch. Neither of us could say anything.

In his autobiography, Johann Wolfgang von Goethe, the German poet and dramatist, gave this detailed account of the coronation of Francis I on April 3, 1764. This detailed description makes the reader feel like he was there.

> The multitude of richly-dressed attendants and magistrates, the stately throng of nobles riding by, were already strain enough upon the sight; but when the Electoral envoys, the hereditary officers, and last of all, under the richly broidered canopy, born by twelve judges and senators, the Emperor himself, in picturesque attire, and to the left, a little behind him, his son, in Spanish dress, swept majestically by on magnificent caparisoned horses, the sight was completely overwhelming.
>
> One would have liked to have arrested the pageantry for a moment by some magic spell; but the splendour passed on without a pause, and immediately in its wake the crowd poured in like a surging sea.

Richard Nixon described his saddest day when he was boarding the helicopter to leave the White House after his resignation as president. He wrote:

> The memory of that scene for me is like a frame of film forever frozen at that moment: the red carpet, the green lawn, the white house, the leaden sky. The starched uniforms and polished shoes of the honor guard.
>
> The new President and his First Lady, Julie, David, Rose. So many friends. The crowd, covering the lawn, spilling out onto the balconies, leaning out of the windows. Silent, waving, crying.

The elegant curve of the South Portico: balcony above balcony. Someone waving a white handkerchief from the window of the Lincoln Bedroom . . . the flag on top of the house, hanging limp in the windless, cheerless morning.

I raised my arms in a final salute. I smiled. I waved goodbye. I turned into the helicopter, the door was closed, the red carpet was rolled up. The engines started. The blades began to turn. The noise grew until it almost blotted out thought. There was no talk. There were no tears left. I leaned my head back against the seat and closed my eyes. I heard Pat saying to no one in particular, "It's so sad. It's so sad."

13

Be Kind

In the beginning of his next book, after he wrote his autobiography, Oscar Levant was remorseful about things he had said in print about certain people. In regard to the Hollywood star Rosalind Russell, he apologized for what he had written. Then he blew the apology by saying that there was an element of truth in what he had said.

Being kind is like remembering to go to the restroom before leaving a restaurant. You'll never be sorry you did. But if you don't, later on you might regret not having done it.

Throughout the ages, people have appreciated the virtue of kindness. In the sixth century BC, the philosopher Lao Tzu wrote, "Kindness in words creates confidence, kindness in thinking creates profoundness, and kindness in giving creates love."

An ancient Japanese proverb states that one kind word can warm three winter months. And in 1825, Johann Wolfgang von Goethe said that kindness is the golden chain by which society is bound.

Throughout the ages, people have appreciated the virtue of kindness.

In telling your story, make the effort to be kind and sprinkle in nuggets of goodness. This is especially important in writing about your family. With rare exception, we like to propitiate our progenitors.

In writing about an ancestral horse thief, imagination can enhance the old fellow's reputation. His relatives will probably describe him as a successful rancher. Instead of his having ended his life with a rope around his neck, he will be portrayed as a pillar of the church, who died peacefully in bed.

Today, popular writing accepts the practice of letting it all hang out. Loving Dad might be exposed as a tyrant, and Mommy Dearest was a bitch. But when recording the story of your life do not be tempted by this current fad. In writing about others in your memoirs, do not judge them harshly. *De mortuis nil nisi bonum.* Don't kick the dead.

In her excellent autobiography, I think Katharine Graham made a mistake by including too much about her difficult marriage. Regardless of the cause of Philip Graham's disagreeable behavior, it's a fact that he was an inconsiderate husband. For example, even though he was married to one of the most attractive and intelligent women in the nation's capital, he would take his mistress to a newspaper convention and introduce her as "my next wife."

He often embarrassed Katharine by belittling her Jewish father, Eugene Meyer, a noted philanthropist and owner of the *Washington Post.* One day when having lunch with Walter Trohan of the *Chicago Tribune,* Phil Graham said, "How can I be happy, knowing that my children are one-fourth Jewish."

Walter replied, "If your children weren't one-fourth Jewish, you wouldn't be head of the *Washington Post.*"

Katharine Graham's intent might have been to set the

record straight. But I see no need for her great-great-great grandchildren to know that their great-great-great grandfather was such a loser.

I also recommend you take it easy when writing about those whom you think have wronged you. Avoid the temptation of trying to get even, to show yourself as either victim or victor, or to make yourself look good. If you persist in always having the last word, you'll end up a very lonesome person. This also applies to your memoirs.

Benvenuto Cellini's autobiography is filled with his stories of those who tried to take advantage of him, and about how he always came out on top. Here is a detailed account of his feud about one of his masterpieces. After receiving a commission from the Bishop of Salamanca to make a vase for the Pope, he dillydallied so long in completing the vase that the bishop was fit to be tied. Cellini wrote:

> Taking the said vase, the Bishop of Salamanca said roughly, "I swear by God that I will make him wait for payment as long as he has loitered in the making of it." Hearing this I remained most discontented, cursing Spain and all who love it.
>
> There was among the other handsome decorations upon this vase a handle made all in one piece with it being most ingeniously contrived, so that by means of a certain spring it stood straight up over the mouth of the vase. One day the said bishop was proudly displaying this vase of mine to certain of his Spanish nobles. After the said prelate had gone away, it happened that one of the noblemen was manipulating too roughly the beautiful handle of the vase. The

delicate spring was unable to resist his uncouth violence and broke off in the hand of the said man.

The bishop had his servant return the vase for Cellini to fix it. Later when the servant came back to get the repaired work of art, Cellini refused to give it to him. He wrote:

The said servant flew into such a rage, that with one hand he made as though he would draw his sword, and with the other made an attempt to enter my shop by force; which I immediately prevented his doing with my own weapon, accompanied by many angry words, saying, "I will not give it to you; and go tell my lord, your master, that I want the money for my labors before it goes out of the shop."

The Spanish bishop finally asked Cellini to meet with him. And this is Cellini's gloating conclusion to this incident:

The bishop's anger gave signs of increasing the more; and having directed them to bring me writing materials, he told me to write under my own hand, saying that I was well content and paid by him. At this I raised my head and said that I would very willingly do so, if first of all I had my money.
The bishop's anger increased and his threats and abuses were terrible. In the end I first received my money, then I wrote the receipt, and departed happy and content.

In writing of her days as prime minister, even though

she was not a great admirer of Jimmy Carter, Margaret Thatcher was kind when she wrote:

> Soon after my arrival (in Tokyo) I went to see President Carter at the United States Embassy, where we talked over our approach to the issues which would arise. Ms. Carter and Amy joined us at the end of the meeting. In spite of press criticism, the Carters obviously enjoyed having their daughter traveling with them—and why not, I thought.
>
> It was impossible not to like Jimmy Carter. He was a deeply committed Christian and a man of obvious sincerity. He was also a man of marked intellectual ability with a grasp, rare among politicians, of science and the scientific method. But he had come into office as the beneficiary of Watergate rather than because he had persuaded America of the rightness of his analysis of the world around them.
>
> He had an unsure handle on economics and was therefore inclined to drift into a futile ad hoc interventionism when problems arose. He found himself surprised and embarrassed by such events as the Soviet invasion of Afghanistan and Iran's seizure of American diplomats as hostages.
>
> And in general he had no large vision of America's future so that, in the face of adversity, he was reduced to preaching the austere doctrine of limits to growth that was unpalatable, even alien, to the American imagination.
>
> In addition to these political flaws, he was in some ways personally ill suited for the presidency,

agonizing over big decisions and too concerned with detail. Finally he violated Napoleon's rule that generals should be lucky. His presidency was dogged with bad luck from OPEC to Afghanistan. What it served to demonstrate, however, was that in heading a great nation decency and assiduousness are not enough.

Having said which, I repeat that I liked Jimmy Carter; he was a good friend to me and to Britain; and if he had come to power in the different circumstances of the post-Cold War world, his talents might have been more apposite.

Do not overlook being kind to yourself. Don't go into detail in describing all of your psychological problems. It's permissible, however, to mention a few symptoms so that future psychiatrist historians can have fun trying to analyze you.

In his autobiography written five hundred years ago, Geronimo Cardano did something unusual. He gave this remarkably honest and detailed portrait of himself.

I, for a man of medium height, my feet are short, wide near the toes and rather too high at the heels, so that I can scarcely find well-fitting shoes; it is usually necessary to have them made to order.

A neck a little long and inclined to be thin, cleft chin, full pendulous lower lip, and eyes that are very small and apparently half-closed. Over the eyebrow of my left eye is a blotch or wart, like a small lentil, which can scarcely be noticed. The wide forehead is bald at the side where it joins the temple.

My hair and beard were blonde. I am wont to go rather closely clipped. The beard, like my chin, is divided, and the part of it beneath my chin always was thick and long.

A rather too shrill voice draws upon me the censure of those who pretend to be my friends, for my tone is harsh and high; yet when I am lecturing, it cannot be heard at any distance. I am inclined to speak in the least suavely, and I speak too often.

I have a fixed gaze as if in meditation; my complexion varies from white to red. An oval face, not too well filled out, the head shaped off narrowly behind and delicately rounded, complete a picture so truly commonplace that several painters who have come from afar to make my portrait have found no feature by which they could so characterize me that I might be distinguished.

Being kind makes humans human. And in writing your autobiography you are image building. When you record with kindness your memory of others and of yourself, you will give the impression of having been an interesting and fair person. That's not all bad.

14

Reflections

Your theme of living will be evident as it flows throughout your story. The force of your unified principles has been the activator of your achievements. For that reason, you should consider telling about the inner stuff that has determined your decisions and actions. Queen Elizabeth II described this as mulling over with the hinter part of her head.

In compiling your reflections, you can include your observations and thoughts about what you consider important. For many years, you've related your life to the world around you. Now you can interpret it as you like. It's your show.

In his autobiography, Benjamin Franklin instructed us how to do good, how to be happy, and how the dance should be danced. With no need for modesty, he considered himself to be living proof of his doctrine. He wrote:

> Before I enter upon my public appearance in business, it may be well to let you know the then state of my

For many years, you've related your life to the world around you.

mind with regard to my principles and morals, that you may see how far those influenced the future events of my life. From the poverty and obscurity in which I was born and in which I passed my earliest years, I have raised myself to a state of affluence and some degree of celebrity in the world.

In telling of his successful battle with cancer, Lance Armstrong wrote:

How do you confront your own death? Sometimes I think the blood-brain barrier is more than just physical, it's emotional, too. Maybe there's a protective mechanism in our psyche that prevents us from accepting our mortality unless we absolutely have to.

The night before brain surgery, I thought about death. I searched out my larger values, and I asked myself, if I was going to die, did I want to do it fighting and clawing or in peaceful surrender? What sort of character did I hope to show? Was I content with myself and what I had done with my life so far?

During the 1970s when the Soviets occupied Czechoslovakia, Vaclav Havel was imprisoned three times. After his final release, he wrote:

When I got out again (in 1983), I suddenly realized that I would probably never write anything about prison. It's hard to explain why this is; certainly not because my memories of this dark period in my life are too painful or depressing, or because they would open old wounds. I think there is a whole set of different reasons behind it.

In the first place, I'm not a narrative writer; I can't write stories, and always forget them *anyway*. In the second place, life outside keeps me too busy, and too frequently comes at me with themes of its own, which I experience directly, immediately, right now. It leaves me no time to return to the utterly different and remote world of my years in prison.

This world is fading from sight behind a strange haze, and everything in it is blending together in a vague and incommunicable dream. I don't feel a vital need to say anything about it. It seems to belong to a personal experience, too much to the past and I'm too preoccupied with the present to be able to go back or produce a sustained evocation of something that was.

In the third place, the most important thing about it is incommunicable. No, I mean it; it was a deeply existential and deeply personal experience, and as such, I'm simply unable to pass it on.

In telling the story of his life, Frederick Douglass reflected on his feelings when he was no longer a slave. He stated:

I have been frequently asked how I felt when I found myself in a free State. I have never been able to answer the question with any satisfaction to myself.

It was a moment of the highest excitement I ever experienced. I suppose I felt as one may imagine the unarmed mariner to feel when he is res-cued by a friendly man-of-war from the pursuit of a pirate.

In writing to a dear friend, immediately after my arrival at New York, I said I felt like one who had escaped a den of hungry lions. This state of mind, however, very soon subsided, and I was again seized with a feeling of great insecurity and loneliness.

The motto which I adopted when I started from slavery was this: "Trust no man!" I saw in every white man an enemy, and in almost every colored man cause for distrust.

At the end of her autobiography, Lillian Hellman, noted playwright, gives an interesting summation of her thoughts. This was the conclusion of her observations:

But I am not yet old enough to like the past bet-ter than the present, although there are nights when I have a passing sadness from the unnec-essary pains, the self-made foolishness that was, is, and will be.

I do regret that I have spent too much *of my* life trying to find what I called "truth," trying to find what I called "sense." I never knew what I meant by truth, never made the sense I hoped for. All I mean is that I left too much of me unfin-ished because I wasted too much time. However—.

In 1666, John Bunyan used his reflections to confess his virtues. Beware of doing this. Remember Shakespeare's

line in *Hamlet,* "The lady doth protest too much, methinks."
Bunyan, who boasted of his modesty, wrote:

> And in this I admire the wisdom of God, that He
> made me shy of women from my first conver-
> sion until now. Those know, and can also bear
> me witness, with whom I have been most inti-
> mately concerned, that it is a rare thing to see
> me carry it pleasant towards a woman, the com-
> mon salutation of a woman I abhor, it is odious
> to me in whosoever I see it.
>
> Their company alone, I cannot away with. I
> seldom so much as touch a woman's hand, for I
> think these things are not so becoming me. When
> I have seen good men salute those women that
> *they* have visited, or that have visited them, I have
> at times made my objection against it, and when
> they have answered that it was but a piece of
> civility, I have told them it is not a comely sight;
> some indeed have urged the holy kiss but then I
> have asked why they made baulks, why they did
> salute the most handsome, and let the ill-favoured
> go; thus, how laudable soever such things have
> been in the eyes of others, they have been un-
> seemly in my sight.
>
> And now for a wind-up in this matter, I call
> not only men, but angels, to prove me guilty of
> having carnally to do with any woman save my
> wife, nor am I afraid to do it a second time, know-
> ing that I cannot offend the Lord in such a case,
> to call God for a record upon my soul, that in
> these things I am innocent.

John Bunyan's quaint way of expressing himself might

be misconstrued as saying, "I have not sinned, and I don't intend to do it again."

Playwright Moss Hart enjoyed reflection on his love of Broadway. He wrote:

> I have thought it fitting to begin this book with my first glimpse of Broadway, since I have spent most of my adult working life in and about its gaudy locale, and if this opening and anecdote falls too quickly into the time-honored tradition of theatrical memoirs, then let the unwary reader beware at the very outset—these annals are not for those unsentimental about the theatre or untouched by its idiocies as well as its glories.

In the seventeenth century, while he was imprisoned and awaiting execution in the Tower of London, King Charles I had much time for reflection. He wrote:

> The solitude and captivity, to which I am now reduced, gives me leisure enough to studie the world's vanities and inconstancie. No restraint shall ensnare my soul in sinne, nor gain that of me, which may make my enemies more insolent, my friends ashamed, or my name accursed. They have no great cause to triumph, that they got my person into their power, since my soul is still my own; nor shall they ever gain my consent against my conscience.
>
> After-time may see what the blindness of this age will not, and God may at length shew my subjects that I chose rather to suffer for them, than with them; happily I might redeem my self to some shew of libertie if I would consent to

enslave them; I had rather hazard the ruine of one King than to confirm many tyrants over them; from whom I pray God deliver them, whatever becomes of me whose solitude hath not left me alone.

When winding up my autobiography *Southern Boy*, I tried to recall my thoughts during World War II. I wrote:

Those of us in the squadron had an amazing way of thinking. In the first place, we were fighting a gentleman's war. We would fly to the battle and then hope to return to our island paradise with comfort, good food, entertainment, a resort-quality beach and a peaceful view of the distant mountains. It was a good life.

Even when we dropped frag (fragmentation) bombs on enemy ground troops, it never occurred to me that I was killing ordinary people like us. I didn't consider that the victims might be sons, husbands and fathers or possibly even college students. They were Germans—the enemy who had to be destroyed before they destroyed us.

The frag bombs we dropped were deadly. They were designed so that when they hit the ground, they would blast off like a mass of hand grenades. On one particular frag mission, we took pride in being credited with having killed 5,000 Germans—that is, 5,000 enemies.

In the account of his life, Colin Powell shares these thirteen rules he has tried to follow:

1. It ain't as bad as you think. It will look better in the morning.
2. Get mad, then get over it.
3. Avoid having your ego so close to your position that when your position falls, your ego goes with it.
4. It can be done!
5. Be careful what you choose. You may get it.
6. Don't let adverse facts stand in the way of a good decision.
7. You can't make someone else's choices. You shouldn't let someone else make yours.
8. Check small things.
9. Share credit.
10. Remain calm. Be kind.
11. Have a vision. Be demanding.
12. Don't take counsel of your fears or naysayers.
13. Perpetual optimism is a force multiplier.

In telling your personal history, it is only right for you to record your own valuable observations and findings. The lessons you have learned from living are ageless. Therefore, your reflections will be of interest and will serve as a guide for those behind you. Let them realize that old can be good—that there is wisdom in the past.

Soon, they too will be next in line.

15

Finale

$\mathbf{Y}$our life deserves to be known and remembered. Your recording of it will be one of your most important accomplishments. By doing it, you will have established a treasured dialogue between yesterday and today. And the past you remember and record will be devoid of time.

Your memoirs prove that you have lived your dream with drive and zest. For others, it will be a delightful kaleidoscope—a documentary with multicolored images.

Completing an autobiography is a winning achievement. As author, you are the first winner. In revisiting each phase of your life, you revive faded memories—many still sweet to the taste. Also, with mature insight, you can better interpret and appreciate past experiences. Although you can't turn back the clock, you will have rewound it.

The other winners are those who will read your story. Understanding the immediate past helps people to interpret the present. It can also make one better prepared for the future.

Completing an autobiography is a winning achievement.

In many ways, your having completed this writing will be cause for celebration. It will be a party for you and your family and friends. With your autobiography in print, you will be extending an open invitation for others to enjoy sharing your life.

As living is a process of continuous growth, you won't run out of source material for updating your autobiography until your last heartbeat. There is a constant unfolding both of images that reappear and of that which is new. So, keep the door open for continuous writing about yourself.

When you look back over your shoulder, you will be satisfied, knowing you have recorded your best. As next in line, you have stepped forward and done your duty. You have become a good example for those standing behind you, waiting their turn.

In a broad sense, telling about your life reaffirms the nobility of man.

Appendix

Authors Quoted

Peter Abelard
Henry Adams
George E. Allen
Lance Armstrong
Saint Augustine
Jimmy Buffett
John Bunyan
Gaius Julius Caesar
Geronimo Cardano
Fidel Castro
Jimmy Carter
Benvenuto Cellini
Charles (Charlie) Chaplin
King Charles I
Colley Cibber
Frederick Douglass
Isadora Duncan
Abba Eban
Dwight D. Eisenhower
Benjamin Franklin
Mohandas K. Gandhi
Henry Louis Gates, Jr.

John Glenn
Johann Wolfgang von
   Goethe
Jane Goodall
Billy Graham
Katharine Graham
Ulysses S. Grant
Moss Hart
Vaclav Havel
Lillian Hellman
Katharine Hepburn
P. D. James
Thomas Jefferson
C. G. Jung
Hellen Keller
Margery Kempe
Martin Luther King, Sr.
Stephen King
Oscar Levant
H. L. Mencken
John Henry
Cardinal Newman

Richard Nixon   Margaret Thatcher
Laurence Olivier   Walter Trohan
Saint Patrick   Anthony Trollope
Samuel Pepys   Mark Twain
Colin Powell   Elie Wiesel
Monty Roberts   Frank Lloyd Wright
Jean Jacques Rousseau   Xenophon

Chronological List of Autobiographies
(by date of writing)

401 BC   Xenophon. *Anabasis, The Expedition of Cyrus into Persia and the Return of the Ten Thousand Greeks.* (Longman, Hurs, Rees, Ormes, Brown & Green, 1824).

58 BC   Julius Caesar. *Caesar's Commentaries.* (Penguin Books, 1981).

400 CE   Saint Augustine. *The Confessions of St. Augustine.* (New City Press, 1996).

440   Saint Patrick. *The Confessions of St. Patrick.* Translated from the Latin by Ludwig Bieler.

1140   Peter Abelard. *History of My Misfortunes.* (Macmillan, 1972).

1436   Margery Kempe. *The Books of Margery Kempe, (Mystics Quarterly,* March-June 1999).

1576   Geronimo Cardano. *De Vita Propria Liber (The Book of My Life).* Translated by Jerome Cardan. 9J. (M. Dent & Sons, Ltd., 1931).

1558-66   Benvenuto Cellini. *Autobiography of Benvenuto Cellini.* (Dodd, Mead & Mead, 1961).

1649   King Charles I. *The Pourtraicture of His Majesty in His Solitude and Sufferings.* (Printed 1649).

1660 Samuel Pepys. *The Diary of Samuel Pepys.* (Everyman's Library, 1963).

1666 John Bunyan. *Grace Abounding to the Chief of Sinners.* (BiblioBazaar, 2007).

1740 Colley Libber. *An Apology for the Life of Mr. Colley Cibber: Comedian Late Patentee of the Theatre-Royal.* (Printed by John Watts for the Author, London, 1740).

1774 Jean Jacques Rousseau. *The Confessions of Jean Jacques Rousseau.* (Random House, Modern Library Books, 1945).

1779 Benjamin Franklin. *Benjamin Franklin: The Autobiography and Other Writings.* (Signet Classics, Penguin Books, 1961).

1815 Johann Wolfgang von Goethe. *Poetry and Truth from My Own Life.* (George Bell & Sons, 1908).

1820 Thomas Jefferson. *Autobiography by Thomas Jefferson.* (Avalon Project at the Yale Law School, 1996).

1845 Frederick Douglass. *Narrative of the Life of Frederick Douglass: An American Slave.* (Anchor Books, Doubleday & Co., 1963).

1864 Henry Cardinal Newman. *Apologia Pro Vita Sua.* (The Modern Library, 1950).

1885 Ulysses S. Grant. *Personal Memoirs of U. S. Grant.* (Library of America and Viking Press, 1990).

1887 Anthony Trollope. *An Autobiography.* (Oxford University Press, 1980).

1902 Helen Keller. *The Story of My Life.* (Doubleday & Co., 1954).

1906 Henry Adams, *The Education of Henry Adams.* (Penguin Books, 1995).

1911 Mark Twain. *Mark Twain's Autobiography*, two volumes. (Harper & Brothers Publishers, 1924).

1927 Isadora Duncan. *My Life.* (Liveright Publishing Corp., 1955).

1932 Frank Lloyd Wright. *An Autobiography.* (Horizon Press, 1932).

1939 H. L. Mencken. *Happy Days 1880–92.* (New York: Alfred A. Knopf, 1968).

1939 H. L. Mencken. *Thirty-five Years of Newspaper Work: A Memoir.* (Baltimore: The Johns Hopkins University Press, 1994).

1950 George E. Allen. *Presidents Who Have Known Me.* (Simon & Schuster, 1950).

1957 Mohandas K. Gandhi. *The Story of My Experiments with Truth: An Autobiography.* (Greenleaf Books, 1995).

1957 C. G. Jung. *Memories, Dreams, Reflections.* (Pantheon Books, 1973).

1959 Moss Hart. *Act One: An Autobiography by Moss Hart.* (Random House, 1959).

1964 Charles Chaplin. *My Autobiography—Charles Chaplin.* (Simon & Schuster, 1964).

1965 Oscar Levant. *The Memoirs of an Amnesiac.* (G. P. Putnam's Sons, 1965).

1967 Dwight D. Eisenhower. *At Ease: Stories I Tell to Friends.* (Doubleday & Co., 1967).

1969 Lillian Hellman. *An Unfinished Woman: A Memoir.* (Little, Brown & Co., 1969).

1971 Walter Trohan. *Political Animal.* (New York: Doubleday & Co., 1971).

1977 Abba Eban. *Abba Eban: An Autobiography.* (New York: Random House, 1977).

1978 Richard Nixon. *The Memoirs of Richard Nixon.* (Grosset & Dunlap, 1978).

1979 Margaret Thatcher. *The Downing Street Years.* (HarperCollins Publishers, 1993).

1980 Reverend Martin Luther King, Sr. *Daddy King, An Autobiography: The Rev. Martin Luther King Sr.* (William Morrow & Co., 1980).

1982 John Glenn. *John Glenn: A Memoir.* (Bantam Books, 1982).

1982 Laurence Olivier. *Confessions of an Actor.* (London: Weidenfeld & Nicholson, 1982).

1985 Fidel Castro. *My Early Years.* (Ocean Press, 1998).

1991 Vaclav Havel. *Disturbing the Peace.* (Viking Books, 1991).

1991 Katharine Hepburn. *Me, Stories of My Life.* (Alfred A. Knopf, 1991).

1994 Henry Louis Gates, Jr. *Colored People: A Memoir.* (Alfred A. Knopf, 1994).

1995 Colin Powell. *My American Journey.* (New York: Random House, 1995).

1995 Elie Wiesel. *All Rivers Run to the Sea: Memoirs.* (Alfred A. Knopf, 1995).

1996 Monty Roberts. *The Man Who Listens to Horses.* (Ballantine Books, 1997).

1997 Billy Graham. *Just As I Am.* (Harper San Francisco, Zondervan, 1997).

1997 Katharine Graham. *Personal History.* (Alfred A. Knopf, 1997).

1998 Jimmy Buffett. *Jimmy Buffett: A Pirate Looks at Fifty.* (Random House, 1998).

1999 Lance Armstrong. *It's Not About the Bike.* (New York: G. P. Putnam's Sons, 2000).

1999 P. D. James. *Time To Be In Earnest.* (Alfred A. Knopf, 1999).

1999 Jane Goodall. *Reason for Hope: A Spiritual*

Journey. (Warner Books, 1999).

2000   Stephen King. *On Writing.* (Scribner, 2000).

2000   Jimmy Carter. *An Hour Before Daylight.* (Simon & Schuster, 2001).

Other Recommended Autobiographies

Jane Adams, *Twenty Years at Hull House*

Michael J. Arlen, *Passage to Ararat*

Russell Baker, *Growing Up*

Thomas Beer, *The Mauve Decade*

S. N. Behrman, *People in a Diary: A Memoir*

John Berryman, *The Freedom of the Poet*

Emily Carr, *Klee Wyck*

Jill Ker Conway, *The Road from Coorain*

Malcolm Cowley, *Exile's Return*

Sammy Davis, Jr., *Yes, I Can*

Annie Dillard, *An American Childhood*

Kildare Dobbs, *Running to Paradise*

Theodore Dreiser, *Dawn*

A. B. Facey, *A Fortunate Life*

B. Anne Walker Fearn, *My Days of Strength*

Paul Fussell, *The Great War & Modern Memory*

Maxim Gorky, *My Childhood*

Robert Graves, *Goodbye to All That*

Graham Greene, *A Sort of Life*

Dick Gregory, *Nigger*

Mrs. Aeneas Gunn, *We of the Never-Never*

Alice Hamilton, *Exploring the Dangerous Trades: The Autobiography of Alice Hamilton, M.D.*

Sir Keith Hancock, *Country or Calling*

Michael Herr, *Dispatches*

Paul Horgan, *Tracings: A Book of Partial Portraits*
John Houseman, *Run-Through: A Memoir*
Maureen Howard, *Facts of Life*
Nikoa Kazantzakis, *Report to Greco*
David Kidd, *Peking Story*
Maxine Hong Kingston, *The Woman Warrior*
C. S. Lewis, *Surprised by Joy*
Robert Lowell, *Life Studies*
Malcolm X, *The Autobiography of Malcolm X*
Beryl Markham, *West With the Night*
Mary McCarthy, *Memoirs of a Catholic Childhood*
Ved Mehta, *Vedi*
Thomas Merton, *Seven Story Mountain*
John Mortimer, *Clinging to the Wreckage: A Part of a Life*
Edwin Muir, *An Autobiography*
Vladimir Nabokov, *Speak, Memory*
Pablo Neruda, *Memoirs*
Iris Origo, *Images and Shadows: Part of a Life*
John Cowper Powys, *Autobiography*
V. S. Pritchett, *A Cab at the Door*
Marcel Proust, *Remembrance of Things Past*
Antoine de Saint-Exupery, *Wind, Sand and Stars*
Jean-Paul Sartre, *The Words*
Seigfried Sassoon, *Memoirs of an Infantry Officer*
Eric Sevareid, *Not So Wild a Dream*
Wilfred Sheed, *Frank and Maisie*
Vincent Sheen, *Personal History*
Kate Simon, *Bronx Primitive*
Eileen Simpson, *Poets in Their Youth*
Lincoln Steffens, *The Autobiography of Lincoln Steffens*
John Steinbeck, *Travels with Charley*
Louis Thomas, *The Younger Science*
James Thurber, *The Years with Ross*

Leo Tolstoy, *Childhood, Boyhood, Youth*

Mary Heaton Vorse, *Time and the Town: A Provincetown Chronicle*

Booker T. Washington, *Up from Slavery*

Ethel Waters, *His Eye Is on the Sparrow*

Theodore H. White, *In Search of History*

Edmund Wilson, *The Twenties*

Edward O. Wilson, *Naturalist*

Leonard Woolf, *Growing: An Autobiography of the Years 1903–11*

W. B. Yeats, *Autobiographies*

O 1/10